The Correction of Taste

On the Late Novels of Henry James

The Correction of Taste

Denis Donoghue

Foreword by Colm Tóibín

THE LILLIPUT PRESS
DUBLIN

First published 2025 by
THE LILLIPUT PRESS
62–63 Sitric Road,
Arbour Hill,
Dublin 7,
Ireland
www.lilliputpress.ie

A CIP record for this title is available from The British
Library.

Hardback ISBN 978 1 84351 946 1
eBook ISBN 978 1 84351 947 8

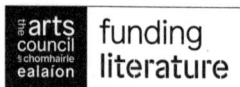

the arts
council
s chomhairle
ealaíon

funding
literature

Set in 11 pt on 17 pt Adobe Caslon Pro by Sarah McCoy
Cover Design by Sarah McCoy
Printed and bound in Czechia by Finidr

Contents

Foreword – Colm Tóibín   *1*

Introduction   25

Henry James and the Great Tradition   58

The Sacred Fount   101

The Wings of the Dove   140

The Ambassadors   183

The Golden Bowl   217

The Sense of the Past   246

The Ivory Tower   265

Afterword – Melissa Malouf   *271*

Endnotes   *275*

This book is dedicated to
Denis Donoghue (1928-2021)
with loving gratitude for all the ways,
for all of us, you pushed the boat out.

Foreword

Colm Tóibín

The man who came to the podium in the large modern lecture hall at University College Dublin in October 1972 was exceedingly tall. He seemed steely and distant and formidable. Despite his name, which was an ordinary southern Irish name, his aura bore the hallmark perhaps of a great house, a place of custom and ceremony with a vast library, old books and pictures.

A year later he would write that he had come to believe that each of us, students embarking on the study of English literature, should, before we were allowed into the department, be asked a simple question upon which everything might depend: to name a passage from a poem or a novel or a play which would make our hair stand on end, which would make us shiver. He imagined, with a sense of wondrous disbelief, what would happen should one of us quote these eight lines from John Crowe Ransom's 'The Equilibrists':

> In Heaven you have heard no marriage is,
> No white flesh tinder to your lecheries,
> Your male and female tissue sweetly shaped
> Sublimed away, and furious blood escaped.
>
> Great lovers lie in Hell, the stubborn ones
> Infatuate of the flesh upon the bones;
> Stuprate, they rend each other when they kiss,
> The pieces kiss again, no end to this.

It was hard looking around Theatre M, part of the recently built complex, modern and anodyne, of the Arts Block of University College Dublin, that October morning and studying the students, the accidental and incoherent presences who had left their breakfast tables to come to their first English lecture, and imagining that either the tone or the sentiments in Ransom's poem would have fired them. But all of us, in some way, had been fired by something, some sense of the mystery and beauty of language or some sense of ourselves as readers, or potential readers, to cause us to be here rather than in the science lab cutting up frogs or at the commerce lecture cutting up ledgers.

We lived, some of us anyway, in a state where those eight lines from Ransom, or lines like them, might potentially move us more than we could say, and the gap between that emotion and its due expression would, we would soon learn, be enough to puzzle us and contain us for all of our lives.

The man, the professor, had by this time taken command of the lectern. There must have been a microphone because the hall was very large but I have no memory of his voice as amplified or in any way distorted. I remember only his first words. He began without explanation or introduction:

One evening coming in with a candle I was startled to hear him say a little tremulously, 'I am lying here in the dark waiting for death'. The light was within a foot of his eyes. I forced myself to murmur, 'Oh, nonsense!' and stood over him as if transfixed.

Anything approaching the change that came over his features I have never seen before, and hope never to see again. Oh, I wasn't touched. I was fascinated. It was as though a veil had been rent. I saw on that ivory face the expression of sombre pride, of ruthless power, of craven terror – of an intense and hopeless despair. Did he live his life again in every detail of desire, temptation, and surrender during that supreme moment of complete knowledge? He cried in a whisper at some image, at some vision – he cried out twice, a cry that was no more than a breath –

'The horror! The horror!'

I blew the candle out and left the cabin. The pilgrims were dining in the mess room, and I took my place opposite the manager, who lifted his eyes to give me a questioning glance, which I successfully ignored. He leaned back serene, with that peculiar smile of his sealing the unexpressed depths of his meanness. A continuous shower of small flies streamed upon the lamp, upon the cloth, upon our hands and faces. Suddenly, the manager's boy put his insolent black head in the doorway, and said in a tone of scathing contempt –

'Mistah Kurtz – he dead.'

Denis Donoghue's voice was dramatic but the tone was not declamatory – it allowed for mystery and quietness. The accent might have been Irish, but the pronunciation of some consonants was strange, almost American, but not quite, and not English either. But as he began to speak, having announced that the passage he had just read came from Conrad's *Heart of Darkness*, the accent ceased to matter as much as the vocabulary mattered, the heightened tone, the not reading from a script, the lack of hesitation, thinking aloud as fierce and eloquent activity, and the sense also that this was important – this attempt to analyse and define and almost imitate layers and levels of feeling, of imaginative energy, of tonal nuance.

Donoghue was alert to the idea of the unsayable, as he circled around the idea of language itself as pliable material, all the more beautiful for that and worthy of our full consideration, but yielding at times to further levels of mystery, offering itself up on an altar where sacrifices would be made to the strange God of our yearning who would deliver us – by virtue of the thunderous action of a sentence – ambiguous meaning and a sense of what lurked or crouched beyond meaning.

As the weeks went on, Donoghue's style of delivery could vary. At times, the mystery could be cast aside, the veil lifted, as it were, and a sharp and precise intelligence applied to the actual meaning of a passage. As he went on to deal with the work of D.H. Lawrence and William Faulkner, we learned to pay due attention to the facts and offer due attention to the rational. This lay somehow at the basis of everything and could be appealed to, without warning, while more sensuous and transcendent matters were left aside.

One of the reasons, indeed one of the excuses, which Henry James Senior, the father of the novelist, had offered his neighbours for gathering his young family up in the 1850s in America and taking them constantly to Europe was that their 'sensuous education' was not being properly looked after in the United States. With one or two notable exceptions, all of us listening in Theatre M that year, while having benefitted from as full and plentiful an education as the Republic of Ireland could provide, had not had a sensuous education at all, or anything like one. Indeed, our parents and guardians would have viewed a sensuous education and what it implied with the same level of disapproval as the old Presbyterian William James of Bailieborough and Albany might have felt had he lived to see his fortune squandered thus on his young grandchildren.

This reading in Conrad and Lawrence and Faulkner was for some of us the first serious and concentrated glimpse of a sensuous universe. The weather outside was grey, the campus was not beautiful. There was, as far as I remember, not a single painting or print to lighten the concrete. The lake in front of the library was said to be ornamental, but it was in fact brutal. Thus the striving of Ursula Brangwen in *The Rainbow* and *Women in Love* for a transforming glimpse of another universe, with other knowledge tempered by the body's radiance, her hunger for possibility against the dullness and the brutality of what was fixed and finite and offered to her, was our striving too against our background, our hunger, and was our reason for being here.

In that same month, October 1972, when Denis Donoghue gave the T.S. Eliot lectures under the title 'Thieves of Fire' at the University of Kent, he alluded to the drama and the extent of Ursula's desires and quoted from Lawrence's version of this: 'In coming out and earning her own living she had made a strong, cruel move towards freeing herself. But having more freedom she only became more profoundly aware of the big want. She wanted so many things. She wanted to read great, beautiful books, and be rich with them; she wanted to see beautiful things, and have the joy of them forever; she wanted to know big, free people; and there remained always the want she could put no name to.'

In that season, the autumn of 1972, some of us learned to the tune of certain lectures on what was then called the modern novel that the last-mentioned want, the one which Ursula could put no name to, was not an ignoble condition, nor a fleeting glimpse of something which would not matter, but once it had descended on us, as it did on her, it would have serious implications; it would mean that we could not go home again, or if we did, having been brushed by the wings of thinking itself as a sensuous activity, we could not sit easily at the family table.

Home for me was Enniscorthy, fourteen or fifteen miles south of Tullow, where Denis Donoghue had been born. An aunt of mine lived close to Tullow and my grandmother had been born not far away, so we often passed through the town, driving along the Slaney to Bunclody and then to Kildavin.

In one of those weekends at home in my first term at University College Dublin, Denis Donoghue's origins in the town of Tullow were casually mentioned by my mother, and the fact that my aunt had briefly done a line, which was the phrase used at the time, with his brother was added as an afterthought. This seemed strange to me and I remember asking if the Donoghues were not rich, from one of the big houses along the valley, and I remember my mother saying that she did not think so.

I learned that a poem was a living thing, not merely a form of action but close to being the performer of an action. I have Denis Donoghue's voice in my mind as I write this. He is saying: 'A poem does not mean; a poem does.' This was a course on the short poem in the sixteenth century. He began once more by reciting. When he had finished, he remarked – and this caused much wonder – 'That is the most erotic poem in the English language':

They flee from me that sometime did me seek
With naked foot stalking in my chamber.
I have seen them gentle, tame, and meek
That now are wild and do not remember
That sometime they put themselves in danger
To take break at my hand; and now they range
Busily seeking with a continual change.

Thanked be fortune it hath been otherwise
Twenty times better, but once in special,
In thin array after a pleasant guise,
When her loose gown from her shoulders
did fall
And she me caught in her arms long and small,
Therewithal sweetly did me kiss
And softly said, 'Dear heart, how like you this?'

It was no dream: I lay broad waking.
But all is turned thorough my gentleness
Into a strange fashion of forsaking.
And I have leave to go of her goodness
And she also to use newfangleness.
But since that I so kindly am served
I would fain know what she hath deserved.

It was made clear to us that we were nothing except intelligent readers as we read this poem – not gay or straight, not male or female, not Irish or English, not black or white, not colonized or rich on the spoils of colony. The words alone worked wonders. It made no difference that some of those poets, including Edmund Spenser and Walter Raleigh, statesmen and soldiers as well as poets, had come to Enniscorthy in the age of Elizabeth with swords, that they had cleared the forests and come to possess vast tracts of land.

We were too busy then – too concerned with tone and style, with plainness and the ornate, with rhyme schemes, with a raw poetry of state- ment in a language that was newly stately, in stanza forms and sonnet shapes – to be inter- rupted by a voice from home whispering that these were the very soldiers who had disfigured Ireland, whose very skills at verse had created categories of the civilized and the barbarian in which they belonged to the former and we, or people like us, were consigned to the latter.

In that year when I was eighteen years old, then, a miracle happened. These poems were handed to me as though they belonged to me; the tradition they came from, their style, the differences and correspondences between them, how the short poem developed in eloquence and tone and balance from decade to decade in the late sixteenth century, the very language they were written in, all of this was handed to me without irony or any questioning. My soul did not fret in their shadow. They were nobody's before they were mine. I had all rights to the English lyric.

I wonder if we were among the last sets of students who were given such freedom – the freedom to cast aside our own history, the history of our country and its anxieties, our own uneven personalities, what set us apart – before these very freedoms began to seem like blinkered restrictions. It made a difference to me that I saw these poems and novels as pure – it was a kind of gift – before I had to re-imagine them in other ways.

/

O city, city! The 10 bus waited on the Belfield campus to take us into Dublin city centre, and there was a wonderful feeling in those years as you dismounted in Leeson Street or Lower Pembroke Street of having the city to yourself while your fellow students suffered under the new suburban dispensation in Belfield. That walk from St Stephen's Green to Grafton Street or to Kildare Street belongs to mythology. It is by making that walk that we remade ourselves.

> Welt, ich bleibe nicht mehr hier,
> Hab ich doch kein Teil an dir,
> Das der Seele könnte taugen.

Denis Donoghue walked each day in the last years of the 1940s from Earlsfort Terrace, the then home of University College Dublin, across Stephen's Green and then down Kildare Street, into the National Library at a time when it was still used by clerks and accountancy students, as it was when I started to read there in 1974, as it had been during the life of W.B. Yeats.

Yeats in his foreword to *Letters from the New Island* remembered that in the National Library 'everybody was working for some examination, nobody, as I thought, for his own mind's sake or to discover happiness'. Yeats remembered looking with scorn 'at those bowed heads and busy eyes, or in futile revery listening to my own mind as if to the sounds in a sea shell'.

Like Yeats, and indeed like Stephen Dedalus, Denis Donoghue must have stood sheltering from the rain under the portico of the National Library before setting out on the next part of his odyssey to South Leinster Street and then Lincoln Place, past Sweny's chemists and then into Westland Row for his singing lesson with Brian Boydell.

Boydell, the composer and teacher, was, Denis Donoghue later wrote, 'a distinguished presence', as indeed he must have been for anyone from an ordinary house in an Irish provincial town. Boydell, Donoghue remembered, 'had no authority, power or any evident desire to govern. His social class – Anglo-Irish Protestant, mercantile rather than aristocratic but bohemian in tone – was in decline, displaced by the new Catholic middle-class politicians who continue to run the country. Boydell had no power, only the prestige of being a musician and a colourful personage.'

In Dublin, music became a surrogate power; training the voice became a way of remaking the self. In this very Westland Row, Leopold Bloom remembered Molly singing Rossini's 'Stabat Mater'. 'Music they wanted. Footdrill stopped. Could hear a pin drop. I told her to pitch her voice against that corner. I could feel the thrill in the air, the full, the people looking up.'

Less than half a century later in the same street, Brian Boydell was working with his pupil Denis Donoghue on an aria from a Bach cantata:

> Welt, ich bleibe nicht mehr hier,
> Hab ich doch kein Teil an dir,
> Das der Seele könnte taugen.

'I suppose,' Donoghue wrote in his book *Speaking of Beauty*, Boydell's

> love of the music and his zeal in leading me through its difficulties implied the beauty he let otherwise speak for itself. We studied

mainly songs of Schubert, Schumann, Brahms – 'Wie bist du meine Koenigin' – and Hugo Wolf, but we also spent many arduous weeks on Bach. The main problem was the frailty of my breathing, a defect especially dramatic in attempting Bach's 'Es ist vollbracht' and, from Cantata 82, 'Ich habe genug', which includes the most beautiful aria I have ever heard, 'Schlummert ein'. Now when I listen to Hans Hotter's recording of it, the music seems to sing itself. Hotter commits his feeling to its determination by the musical line; he never asserts himself or challenges the authority of the phrases … Boydell tried hard to show me how to save my breath for the lines:

Welt, ich bleibe nicht mehr hier,
Hab ich doch kein Teil an dir,
Das der Seele konnte taugen

but I never reached 'taugen' with more than a whisper left.

/

The four pillars of the edifice that Denis Donoghue created were W.B. Yeats, T.S. Eliot, Henry James and Wallace Stevens. When I asked him once what impact reading Stevens had had on his life, he told me that it changed everything, how he saw things, but also how he wrote, adding that both he and Frank Kermode had agreed that they could no longer write the same type of sentences once they had immersed themselves in Stevens. The American poet gave this Irishman and Englishman permission to write more gorgeously, to take greater risks with cadences. Donoghue's own personal copy of Stevens's *Collected Poems* was fully annotated, with cross-references to other poems by Stevens, to the poet's essays and letters, to the books he had been reading.

'But it was Stevens's music I most wanted to hear,' Donoghue wrote in a preface to the 1983 edition of his *Connoisseurs of Chaos: Ideas of Order in American Poetry*. In that preface he offered a picture of the strange and limited conditions under which he began as a writer in Dublin about American literature. In his memoir

Warrenpoint, he set out the atmosphere in which his own growth as an intellectual and a critic had been so unlikely. In his writing about Brian Boydell, he set out his own failure to become a classical singer. In the preface to *Connoisseurs of Chaos*, he wrote: 'When I was an undergraduate at University College Dublin, we had no courses in American literature.' He notes how few American books there were in Dublin libraries.

Donoghue quotes T.S. Eliot on writing and criticism: 'I maintain even that the criticism employed by a trained and skilled writer on his own work is the most vital, the highest kind of criticism, and … that some creative writers are superior to others solely because their critical faculty is superior.'

It was not merely that Donoghue admired Henry James's essays and prefaces as aspects of the novelist's criticism, but he saw James's critical faculty at work in how James, in his fiction, created scenes and characters and outcomes. James had little interest in instinct except when he needed to show how dangerous it could be, how it lay ready to pounce on the most innocent characters, and the most cultivated. He himself, as a novelist, could judge it and control it, while keeping it at bay.

With the publication of Eve Sedgwick's *Epistemology of the Closet* in 1990, the study of Henry James in universities was transformed. No longer was he the exquisite figure, the master of style, the artist who avoided politics and the general mess out there and allowed his exalted, refined and privileged characters to live outside society or history, and whose sexual feelings were repressed or filled with guilt and secrecy and expressed most forcefully by means of the gaze or the high tone of renunciation.

Sedgwick saw James as a repressed homo-sexual and believed his work was saturated with images of hidden desire and sexual desperation. She did not seek to diminish James; in fact, her book created a new appetite for the study of his work.

In some ways, Denis Donoghue's writing about late James in *The Correction of Taste* inhab-its a critical moment between F.R. Leavis's 'ethical sensibility' and Eve Sedgwick's work on sexual neurosis, but does so in terms that are set by neither, but by Donoghue's skill as an interpreter and by his own vision of life.

A few times in the book, Donoghue nods in the direction of the future. 'If Henry James,' he writes, 'and Jocelyn Persse [a close friend of James, a nephew of Lady Gregory] had been born well over a century later, they could have had a same-sex marriage. Or not. Probably not, if James's sometimes self-defeating tastes were to be consulted. He wouldn't allow himself the pleasures he denies so many of the characters in his major stories and novels.'

When he contemplates the privileged world of James's late novel *The Sacred Fount*, Donoghue points out, echoing Prufrock: 'I am not Terry Eagleton, nor was meant to be.' It is with gentle irony rather than high indignation that he ends this passage with what is missing, mostly, in James's work: 'Not a word about the other marvel of civilized life, provided by the gardeners, housekeepers, maids, footmen who carry the suitcases, cleaners, cooks, and other servants who keep the affluence of fine things flourishing.'

A few times also, Donoghue nods to the ghost of Leavis. When he considers Lambert Strether's famous exhortatory remark in *The Ambassadors*, 'Live all you can, it's a mistake not to', he then considers Strether's next phrase, 'It doesn't matter what you do', and feels compelled to write: 'Excuse me, it does.' Leavis would also recognize the tone in a final paragraph on *The Golden Bowl* when Donoghue outlines Maggie Verver's achievement against all the odds: 'It is mostly an edifying spectacle.'

Unlike Leavis and Sedgwick, Donoghue did not have a theory to impose on his reading of a novel. He writes about listening to music: 'When I attend a piano recital, I determine to listen to the music and, as far as possible, to postpone other considerations. They will – or may – insist later.'

In this book, he gives more away than he normally does, including his open enthusiasm for some of these texts. *The Sacred Fount* is, he writes, 'the only novel by Henry James that I have read six times … When I come to Chapter 8, I am not ready to be ravished, as I am when I read "Among School Children" and "Ash Wednesday", but after a few sentences, I give in.'

Once Donoghue has disclosed his feelings, he sets about exercising his intelligence, aware, as he notes, that 'only an alert reader could rise to James's occasions. He is not writing for lazy consumers or for common members of the broad-backed public.'

He then sets about rising to the occasions not of James's famous late style but the occasions when the style fails James or becomes puzzling or indeed soars. It is not a stable thing, style. Nor indeed is narrative structure in these novels or, for that matter, point of view.

Since the three main novels under consideration – *The Ambassadors*, *The Wings of the Dove* and *The Golden Bowl* – are told in the third person, then the question is: what does this do? Donoghue believes the perspectives in *The Ambassadors*, the way in which Strether is implicated in the very telling of the story, require close attention. And then he offers them close attention.

In 1906, when these three novels had been published, Henry James became impatient with his young friend Hendrik Andersen, whose work as a sculptor was not finding favour with buyers: 'You are not even realizing that benefit of friction with the market which is so true a one for solitary artists too much steeped in their mere personal dreams.' James then referred to the need for artists to produce 'the potboiler', and went on: 'the potboiler which represents, in the lives of all artists, some of the most beautiful things ever done by them'.

Donoghue notes the aura of potboiler in the basic plot of these late novels, especially *The Wings of the Dove* and *The Golden Bowl*. He writes about 'the lurid quality' of the story in *The Wings of the Dove*. He then sets out to trace how James rescued these novels from their crude origins through subtlety, tact, ambiguity and sharp intelligence.

Since these qualities are what nourish Donoghue's own procedures, then in this last book of criticism, the style he describes and the cast of mind he summons up appear to have met their match in his own style, his own cast of mind, his own powers of analysis at their most complete.

Introduction

I

I have taken the title of this book from T.S. Eliot's essay 'The Function of Criticism' (1923). But the book is not about him or his work as my *Words Alone* is; it is a reading of Henry James, concentrating on his later fiction. This introduction is designed to enable me to move from Eliot to James without forgetting Eliot's concerns. I have long held that when Eliot settled in London rather than in Boston or Cambridge, Mass., he took upon himself an immense project, nothing less than the conversion of Britain to Anglo-Catholicism and the acceptance of Original Sin as first article of religious belief. Eliot's approval of Hulme's *Speculations* is to be understood in this context. Hopkins's prayer, at the end of 'The Wreck of the Deutschland', suggests itself: 'Our King back, oh, upon English souls!' Inevitably failing in this project, as Hopkins, too, failed, Eliot resorted to a more ascertainable plan, that of improving British manners. One of his motives in assuming the editorship of *The Criterion* was to speak with some authority on cultural issues. He would have to earn that authority, but he hoped to do so – and for a while, he did.

'The Function of Criticism' is a work of angry intelligence, which reads as if it were written under duress. It sounds as if, in writing it, he would have preferred to be writing anything else, or to be silent. He accepts that criticism includes, unfortunately, every form of discursive writing from a brief book review to a supreme work of criticism such as Sainte-Beuve's *Port-Royal*. In 'Tradition and the Individual Talent' (1919) he wrote that 'criticism is as inevitable as breathing', forgetting that breathing is not inevitable but a temporary gift, and he appeared to be unable to think of any good reason why certain critics, unnamed, should be encouraged to keep breathing. In 'Religion and Literature' (1935) he said – in poor taste, admittedly – that we should not leave criticism 'to the fellows who write reviews in the papers'.[1] It is difficult to designate a function for such a fellowship. Given the field of literary criticism in the broadest sense, Eliot would have liked to see most of its wandering inhabitants ejected. In happier conditions, literary criticism would be rarely needed:

> I have had some experience of Extension lecturing, and I have found only two ways of leading any pupils to like anything with the right liking: to present them with a selection of the simpler kind of facts about a work – its conditions, its setting, its genesis – or else to spring the work on them in such a way that they were not prepared to be prejudiced against it. There were many facts to help them with Elizabethan drama: the poems of T.E. Hulme only needed to be read aloud to have immediate effect.[2]

The conditions that obtained in the literary milieu of London and Paris in the early twentieth century prompted Eliot to hold that the best kind of literary criticism arose when a poet applied his most intense critical consciousness to the first drafts of his poem, to make it as good as he could make it on that day. 'I maintain even that the criticism employed by a trained and skilled writer on his own work is the most vital, the highest kind of criticism; and ... that some creative writers are superior to others solely because their critical faculty is superior.'[3] The next best conditions occur when a poet, on request, studies the first drafts of a friend's poem as carefully as if they were his own. Eliot found these agreeable conditions at hand when he asked Ezra Pound to read a long, straggling poem called 'He Do the Police in Different Voices'. Pound's criticism and Eliot's own together turned the straggle into *The Waste Land*.

That felicity rarely came about. When it didn't, Eliot hoped that criticism would be a modest affair and would benefit from that quality: 'And any book, any essay, any note in

Notes and Queries, which produces a fact even of the lowest order about a work of art is a better piece of work than nine-tenths of the most pretentious critical journalism, in journals or in books.'[4] I take some comfort from that sentence. Many years ago I submitted two brief notes to J.C. Maxwell, editor of *Notes and Queries*. He accepted one, rejected the other: not a bad percentage. Eliot enlarged the scope of criticism when he said:

> The critic, one would suppose, if he is to justify his existence, should endeavour to discipline his personal prejudices and cranks – tastes to which we are all subject – and compose his differences with as many of his fellows as possible, in the common pursuit of true judgment.[5]

That phrase, 'the common pursuit', entered into general literary reference when F.R. Leavis used it as the title of a selection of his essays, which in turn became the title of a play about Leavis and his turbulent colleagues in Cambridge.

Eliot is at his angriest in the second section of 'The Function of Criticism', where he is provoked by one of John Middleton Murry's sentences: 'The English writer, the English divine, the English statesman, inherit no rules from their forebears; they inherit only this: a sense that in the last resort they must depend upon the inner voice.'[6] Eliot's reply, which I quote only in part, is a telling instance of his astringency:

> This statement does, I admit, appear to cover certain cases: it throws a flood of light upon Mr. Lloyd George. But why *'in the last resort'*? Do they, then, avoid the dictates of the inner voice up to the last extremity? My belief is that those who possess this inner voice are ready enough to hearken to it, and will hear no other. The inner voice, in fact, sounds remarkably like an old principle which has been formulated by an elder critic in the now familiar phrase of 'doing as one likes.' The possessors of the inner voice ride ten in a compartment to a football match at Swansea, listening to the inner voice, which

breathes the eternal message of vanity, fear, and lust.[7]

It is the old quarrel with Murry about Classicism and Romanticism, but even in anger Eliot's penultimate sentence is distasteful. He avoids naming the elder critic, Matthew Arnold, because he doesn't like to mention him except to point out his errors, and because he wants to keep the focus on Murry; though in passing he strikes a blow with 'an old principle'. 'Ten in a compartment', a crowded third-class carriage, the cheapest seats. It is a blatant lapse of taste on Eliot's part to claim that he knows the eternal message breathed by the inner voice – to which he never listens – 'of vanity, fear, and lust': how would he know these deliverances well enough to distinguish them? Calling the Inner Voice Whiggery, as he does elsewhere, Eliot puts himself under the obligation of justifying his anger. I am expected to know the light that Murry's sentence throws on Lloyd George, but I don't.

Eliot is honour-bound to say what the function of criticism is, however reluctant he is to say that it has one. He drives himself toward the statement by contrasting art and criticism in their different characters, a contrast hardly necessary since no one has ever confounded them:

> No exponent of criticism … has, I presume, ever made the preposterous assumption that criticism is an autotelic activity. I do not deny that art may be affirmed to serve ends beyond itself; but art is not required to be aware of these ends, and indeed performs its function, whatever that may be, according to various theories of value, much better by indifference to them. Criticism, on the other hand, must always profess an end in view, which, roughly speaking, appears to be the elucidation of works of art and the correction of taste.[8]

It is hard to say how roughly the speaking proceeds. Criticism that 'must always profess an end in view' doesn't sound rough or approximate – it knows exactly what it intends to do. Eliot is anxious to attach the hard word 'autotelic' to art and to let criticism do the best it can with its secondary character. Many scholars, including the editors of the *Oxford English Dictionary*, 1991 reprint with corrections, have lived useful lives without needing the word 'autotelic'. In Eliot's passage it has the force of 'No Entry' or 'Keep off the Grass'. It would not have that force if Eliot had lived long enough and acquired the patience to appreciate the criticism – much of it autotelic – of Foucault, Barthes, de Man and Derrida.

But Eliot's double formula is doubtful. I wonder how he would have reacted if someone – I.A. Richards, for instance – had submitted to the editor of *The Criterion* an essay called 'A Further Elucidation of *The Waste Land*'. He might have snorted: '*The Waste Land* does not need to be elucidated, it only needs to be read aloud by a competent speaker, just as I, in my teaching days, read aloud Hulme's "The Embankment"' – a poem prefaced by Hulme with the words, in parenthesis '(The fantasia of a fallen gentleman on a cold, bitter night)':

Once, in finesse of fiddles found I ecstasy,
In the flash of gold heels on the hard
pavement.
Now see I
That warmth's the very stuff of poesy.
Oh. God, make small
The old star-eaten blanket of the sky
That I may fold it round me and in comfort
lie.[9]

If I had read that poem in one of my poetry classes at University College Dublin or later at New York University, I feel sure that three or four students would ask a question along these lines: Isn't this a poem in Free Verse, despite the rhyming of ecstasy, I, poesy, sky and lie? Doesn't Eliot quote it again in his essay on Free Verse? Doesn't he normally affirm that there is no such thing as Free Verse? My answer would begin: No, he doesn't deny that there is Free Verse; he quotes Hulme's 'The Embankment' because of its beauty and because 'the charm of these lines could not be, without the constant suggestion and the skilful evasion of iambic pentameter'.[10]

Note too, I might have added, that the first and last lines have twelve syllables, as if the iambic pentameter were extended by an extra foot. And two of its seven lines are standard iambic pentameters. Why we have 'poesy' instead of 'poetry' would be a good question for the next class.

Eliot does not say what the impact of 'The Embankment' was on the class to which he read it. Perhaps he could not produce evidence, except to say that the poem clearly gave pleasure. Maybe he urged the class to listen as if they were listening to a piece of music. If we have a chance to hear András Schiff playing Bach's *Well-Tempered Clavier*, we do not say anything, unless we are musicologists or professional music critics: anything we could say would be banal, our response not a discursive one. It may be analogous to the experience that Eliot adumbrates at the end of 'The Dry Salvages' of music heard so deeply

> That it is not heard at all, but you are the music
> While the music lasts.[11]

– if such a degree of transformation is possible. This is probably enough to show that 'elucidation' is not quite the right word in Eliot's phrase 'the elucidation of works of art'. By calling works of art 'autotelic', he protected them from bogus intimacy, but he did not say what form a proper relation would take. The *OED* says that to elucidate is 'to throw light upon, to clear up, to explain', but Eliot does not mean that works of art need to be so treated, if they need anything. 'The correction of taste' is more intelligible. I take him to mean that if something is in bad taste it should be corrected by appeal to good taste. Good taste is the custom by which we like something with the right liking. That is the direction of good teaching. The function of criticism – as of good teaching – is to lead students, readers, to like something for the right reason and then to be able to expound that reason.

Some of Eliot's evidences are easy. Take again his sentence about the soccer fans in the train to Swansea. Suppose Eliot, in the company of the upper-middle-class men and women who were his frequent companions, were to speak that sentence about the inner voice, surely someone would protest 'I say, Tom, that's enough if not too much'. That would be an appeal to the imperative of taste. What further penalty would be imposed is hard to say. The sentence would hardly merit Eliot's expulsion from polite society. Is there a lapse of taste in 'Morning at the Window' when Eliot writes: 'I am aware of the damp souls of housemaids / Sprouting despondently at area gates'? How could he be aware of such entities, know them to be damp, see them sprouting and their victims despondent? In 'Sweeney Erect' the ladies of the corridor 'Call witness to their principles / And deprecate the lack of taste'. What they deprecate is the absence of a decent, assured operation of custom in the surrounding social behaviour. As well they might, since this absence compels them to call witness to their principles. Taste, like manners, has no laws to which to appeal, except in social practice. If custom does not operate, the game is lost. But the laws of taste, if there are any, are not universal. They obey the conventions of a social class. If Eliot were thinking of cricket rather than of football and adverted to three or four upper-class men and women going by taxi to the Oval, he would not claim to know the content of their souls or suspect the presence of vanity, fear and lust.

Eliot does not try to define taste. He thinks it sufficient – and he may be right – to let a sense of it emerge from the tone in which he speaks of liking things with the right liking. I should try to be more specific. Taste is a form of pastoral; it tries to run a society by manners and customs, not by laws and traffic lights. Serena Williams and Maria Sharapova are known to dislike each other: there is frost between them. But at the end of a match, no matter who has won, they shake hands and mildly smile. That is the rule of taste, embodied in a well-understood custom. At the US Open in 2019 I saw a winner neglect to shake hands with his opponent. I don't know whether a penalty followed. At the same tournament fines totalling $19,000 were imposed on Daniil Medvedev for misbehaviours that must have been serious. Lapses of taste are usually accommodated without tangible penalty.

Presumably Eliot had in mind, by the correction of taste, occasions on which the exalted sense of a word was presupposed but was then traduced, mocked or parodied. Obscenities are not a problem, so long as they are confined to their low quarters; they become a problem when they are played for after-dinner laughs in drawing room or club. To invoke taste in the high sense, you have to fend off its common-or-vulgar sense. You can't let the word go here and there. You could mispronounce the word, if you wanted to, and make it come out as 'test', as Edmund could when he pretends to keep the letter out of his father's hands (*King Lear* 1.2.44–5). 'I hope, for my brother's justification, he wrote this but as an essay or taste of my virtue.' 'Test' would have nothing to do with the mouth; 'taste' would sound oral, a mouthy word. Hotspur would have no call to mispronounce the word when he shouts the hyperbole

> Come, let me taste my horse,
> Who is to bear me like a thunderbolt
> Against the bosom of the Prince of Wales
> (*1 Henry IV* 4.2.119–21)

II

Why James, who is not regarded as sinning against taste? It would be a waste of my short time to trawl through his collected writings in search of vulgarity. Two instances – of many or few – will do.

When I first read *The Bostonians* (1886), I must have slept through the first chapters, else I would have noted the ugliest, most tasteless sentence in the book. Olive Chancellor has brought Basil Ransom to meet Mrs Farrinder at Miss Birdseye's. She introduces Ransom to Miss Birdseye. I need not quote the whole sentence; this part will be enough. Poor Miss Birdseye 'gave the young man a delicate, dirty, democratic little hand, looking at him kindly, as she could not help doing' (p. 25). This is the narrator speaking. I call him HJ in the slight hope of distinguishing him from Henry James. The quoted sentence is my nomination for the most wretched use of alliteration. I wonder when Miss B's hand got dirty and stayed that way.

The second passage. Here is James, in his twenties, showing off to his family and rude,

writing on 7 and 8 November 1869 from Rome
to his 'Beloved Sister' Alice about Pope Pius IX:

> A glimpse indeed I had some three days
> since, when the Pope came in state to say
> mass at a church opposite this hotel. I made
> no attempt to enter the church: but I saw
> tolerably well the arrival of the cardinals &
> ambassadors & etc, & finally of the Grand
> Llama in person ... When you have seen that
> [bloated] flaccid old woman waving his
> ridiculous fingers over the prostrate multi-
> tude & have duly felt the picturesqueness of
> the scene – & then turn away sickened by its
> absolute *obscenity* – you may climb the steps
> of the Capitol & contemplate the equestrian
> statue of Marcus Aurelius ... As you revert to
> that poor sexless old Pope enthroned upon
> his cushions – & then glance at those impe-
> rial legs swinging in their immortal bronze,
> you cry out that here at least was a *man!*[12]

In 'A Roman Holiday' (1873) – a chapter of
Italian Hours – James refers to 'the Pope sitting

deep in the shadow of his great chariot with uplifted fingers like some inaccessible idol in his shrine'.[13] I don't see any impropriety in the Pope's celebrating Mass in a minor church in Rome and raising his hand – 'ridiculous fingers' – to bless the faithful.

I decided to attempt this book when I was again reading *The Ambassadors* and finding myself disagreeing with the standard reading of that novel, so far as I knew there was such a thing. Often – or often enough – reading James's short stories, I found myself stumped, affronted by a detail that had to be a question of taste, something I could make nothing of. A small example: 'Crapy Cornelia', published in *Harper's Monthly Magazine*, October 1909. The story begins with White-Mason, a bachelor of forty-eight, having taken a walk, now sitting down in Central Park to enjoy the charm of procrastination. Boys and girls are running around; Nature is doing what it usually does on a Wednesday afternoon. When a nearby clock struck 5.30, he knew that he must approach the question of Mrs Worthingham. Three ladies have turned down his proposal of marriage, but he does not feel defeated: he is ready to put the question to Mrs W. Arrived at her house and received, he is struck by the repellent newness of everything, the glitter, the flare, the 'scenic extravagance' of Mrs Worthingham's decor. There is also a third party in the room, a 'dingy' presence whom Mrs W. shows no intention of introducing.

After a while White-Mason recognizes her as Cornelia Rasch, a friend from the dusty past, recently widowed. 'Why, it has been *you* all this time?' he exclaims. 'May I come and see you the very first thing?' 'Yes, you may call – but only when this dear lovely lady has done with you' – surely one of the most tasteful ripostes in James's fiction.[14] Soon after, Cornelia leaves, placing her card, apparently for Mrs Worthingham's convenience, on the hall table. Meanwhile, White-Mason realized that the modern Mrs Worthingham 'had no data':

> He almost hugged the word—it suddenly came to mean so much to him. No data, he felt, for a conception of the sort of thing the

THE CORRECTION OF TASTE

New York of 'his time' had been in his personal life—the New York so unexpectedly, so vividly, and, as he might say, so perversely called back to all his senses by its identity with that of poor Cornelia's time … his time and hers had been the same.[14]

White-Mason, on his way out, looks at the card long enough to make a mental note of Cornelia's address. Leaving Mrs Worthingham's house, he heads back to the park and seats himself.

Three days later he finds himself in Cornelia's little flat, leaning back, stretching his legs and smoking cigarettes before the fire. They talk of gone times, old friends, of Mary Cardew with whom White-Mason may have been in love. The talk is so rich, so consanguineous, that Cornelia is justified in asking him, twice, 'Do you mean you want to marry *me*?' The first time, he is too excited to notice the question. Approaching the second, 'Do you want to marry *me*!' we read:

It had this time better success—if the term may be felt in any degree to apply. All his candour, or more of it at least, was in his slow, mild, kind, considering head-shake. 'No, Cornelia—not to *marry* you.'

Why not? Why on earth not? Cornelia does not ask either of these questions. James gives her a way out:

His discrimination was a wonder, but since she was clearly treating him now as if everything about him was, so she could as exquisitely meet it. 'Not at least,' she convulsively smiled, 'until you've honourably tried Mrs. Worthingham. Don't you really *mean* to?' she gallantly insisted.

Still no reply. 'He waited again a little; then he brought out: "I'll tell you presently."' Whereupon he changes the subject, wandering among old times, photographs, how Mary Cardew dressed. Later, Cornelia reminds him that he had something to tell her. More delay. 'Don't you mean to try—?' 'Mrs. Worthingham?' He pauses, fiddles with his pocketbook. 'Finally he spoke: "No—I've decided. I can't—I don't want to."' Cornelia has only one question left:

'But what—since you can't marry me!—can you do with me?'

Well, he seemed to have it all. 'Everything. I can live with you—just this way.' To illustrate which he dropped into the other chair by her fire; where, leaning back, he gazed at the flame. 'I can't give you up. It's very curious. It has come over me as it did over you when you renounced Bognor.

That's it—I know it at last, and I see one can like it. I'm "high." You needn't deny it. That's my taste. I'm old.' And in spite of the considerable glow there of her little household altar he said it without the scowl.[15]

He had already announced 'I shall turn up here, daily' – not waiting for an invitation. Surely there is a question of taste here, but no easy answer offers itself. The story ends, in the passage I've just now quoted, on what we are to take as a happy ending; but it would be more plausible to take it as a man's peaceful conquest of a woman. One question we can dispose of: marriage. Cornelia expects it and wants it, but there is no proposal.

I've encountered disagreement about that last sentence and the implication that White-Mason has displayed bad taste. Melissa Malouf, my colleague in all things Jamesian, and my partner in all other things, sees the widow Cornelia as quite content to avoid 'more adventures'. She has returned to New York because 'I knew of a sudden one day—knew as never before—that I was old'. White-Mason, himself at forty-eight well on the other side of youthfulness, asks: 'And how do you like it?' Cornelia has the perfect answer: 'Well, if I liked it, it was on the principle on which some people like high game.' White-Mason is delighted: '"High game—that's good!" he laughed. "Ah, my dear, we're 'high'!"'[16] The marriage errand he was on when he paid his visit to Mrs Worthingham now seems silly, she is 'so other!' With Cornelia, the business of marriage is supplanted, for both of them, by the 'taste' – White-Mason's word – of high game: of all that is old about them, their things, their shared memories, their ideas, their crapy clothes. 'Oh, how we can talk!' A marriage of true minds needn't bow its head to the institution of marriage. Cornelia, despite her questions, which arise far more out of curiosity than desire, is at peace with such an arrangement.

Maybe: James's attitude to marriage was volatile. He knew some good ones, starting with his parents and going on to brother William. He knew some bad ones, Edith Wharton's especially. But he suspected marriage as an institution, because like all institutions marriage is – at least in theory – a fixity, a definite incorrigible thing; it laughs at the strivings of the imagination, sends them packing. The trouble with institutions is that they are already there. James's father maintained, in print, that divorce would be justified if the relation between the married partners turned out to be that of cat and dog. James's mother urged him to marry and start a family. Her son let the advice pass by. He tries hard, in several stories, to evade the jingle of wedding bells. White-Mason drops into the chair on the other side of Cornelia's. He does not request; he informs, delivers the social facts he has chosen. I don't know what to make of his intention to tell Cornelia something, followed by his decision not to. I wish she had said 'thanks very much for nothing'. At the end of another of James's short stories, 'Broken Wings', writer Mrs Harvey and painter Stuart Straith, their embrace long because long delayed, don't say: 'let's name the day!' They say: 'And now to work!'

If Henry James and Jocelyn Persse had been born well over a century later, they could have had a same-sex marriage. Or not. Probably not, if James's sometimes self-defeating tastes were to be consulted. He wouldn't allow himself the pleasures he denies so many of the characters in his major stories and novels.

III

James was of course not always in top form when
it came to imagining the complex relations of men
to women, women to women, men to men, especially if we take, as I do, the later great novels as
exemplary. He was capable of writing a tasteless
novel that Leon Edel describes as 'an outburst of
primitive rage that seems irrational and uncontrolled'.[17] *The Other House*, published in 1896, may
not be as bad as all that. Neither is it as good as
Louis Begley claims in his introduction to the
New York Review edition. And then there is
James's own remarkable assessment, in a journal
note of 4 January 1910: 'Oh, blest *Other House*,
which gives me thus at every step a procedure, a
support, a divine little light to walk by.'[18] It is this
assessment that brings me to mention *The Other
House* when it comes to the question of taste.

James was still in his playwriting phase –
approximately 1891–1895 – when he first
imagined *The Other House*. In a detailed journal
note on 26 December 1893, he writes of 'a young
man who has lost his wife, and who has a little

girl, the only issue of that prematurely frustrated union'.[19] Shortly before her death, his wife extracts from him a promise: that he would not marry again. And not just that: he is not to marry again during the lifetime of the child. She demanded this promise because of her 'overwhelming dread of a stepmother'. She had had a stepmother herself 'who rendered her miserable, darkened and blighted her youth'.[20] For five years, according to James, all goes well – 'the husband doesn't think of marrying again'. Then he falls in love with the Good Heroine, and she with him, but the promise is still to be kept. There is another young woman in the vicinity, the Bad Heroine, who is also in love with the Hero, but he is not in love with her. This woman has a serious suitor, a man of means – which matters – but she rejects him. She will have Tony Bream, and in order to have him, the child must die. The Bad Heroine 'determines to poison the child – on the calculation that suspicion will fall on her rival'.[21] At this point in his note, James begins to doubt the denouement. He will have the family doctor somehow intervene, empty a locket containing some toxic liquid. Act II would entail the child nevertheless falling very ill, for which the Good Heroine is blamed. To save her reputation, the Hero claims that he has been responsible for the ailment of the child, but no one believes him because he is universally liked. Act III: blame now falls on the culprit, but it so happens that her suitor has again returned from abroad. He is appalled at what the Bad Heroine has done, but to save her he plucks her up and takes her abroad, if not as far as China, still to some foreign country. After a long and decent interval, the Hero marries the Good Heroine. James was unsuccessful in getting this soap opera onto the stage.

But there was something about this plot, 'a support, a divine little light to walk by', that led James 'to play his cards rapidly here, almost impatiently'[22] and turn to the novel we now have in hand, where it sits uneasily between, say, *The Portrait of a Lady* and *What Maisie Knew*. With the exception of the Good Heroine, Jean Markle, all of the characters in *The Other House* are unattractive, exaggerated, tasteless in their gossipy relations to one another. The hero, Tony Bream, keeps his promise to his dead wife and remains extraordinarily clueless when it comes to the women who are quite ready to marry him. He laughs too much: there is no encounter, until the finale, that doesn't leave him smiling, happy to be handsome Tony, the owner of the 'other house' – other because it is just across the river from Eastmeade, where the interfering Mrs Beever presides over everyone. There is a short walk over a bridge from her 'great, clean, solid square solitude' to the other house.[23] Rose Armiger, fast friend of the now dead Julia Bream, moves with news in hand from one house to the other. Jean Martie is also a visitor – Tony is entranced by her hair – in both locations. Mrs Beever has decided that her dull, heavy son will woo the lovely Jean. Rose Armiger, though she has been courted by Dennis Vidal, wants Tony Bream. The child is in the way.

James has here a cast of central characters who wouldn't know the subtleties of tact if they smacked them in the face. It's as if James is saying to himself, 'I can do *this*, too. I can write about

people who don't know how to censure themselves, when to keep quiet, to swerve, to give up.'
He can write a theatrical, sensational novel. He
can, this time, ignore his initial notes and let
Rose Armiger drown the child. The family
doctor, who discovers the body, explains: 'She
was immersed – she was held under water – she
was made sure of.'[24] And James can make the
suitor who no longer loves Rose be part of the
cover-up: he 'put out a hand and seized her, and
they passed quickly into the night'.[25] Imagine
such a sentence in the later novels! Or this
exchange between Rose and Dennis Vidal:

> 'If I count on you, it's to support me. If I say
> things, it's for you to say them.'

> 'Even when they're black lies?' Dennis
> brought out.

> Her answer was immediate. 'What need
> should I have of you if they were white
> ones?'[26]

Rose Armiger gets away with murder. She had hoped for Jean to be blamed. Instead, Tony confesses in order to protect Jean. The doctor plots to protect Tony – it is he who convinces Dennis to take Rose away.

Protecting the family honour is also in the mix. Only Jean wants to throw caution to the winds: 'I wish to hunt her to death! I wish to burn her alive! … I could tear her limb from limb. That's what she tried to do to me!'[27] Tony is resigned, content to believe that Rose's 'doom will be to live'. Besides, he says a bit later on, 'People won't challenge me.'[28] Everyone likes him too much. He's so handsome. They will sympathize. They will believe the doctor's story that the child died from a sudden 'attack'.

The murder of the child has freed Tony from his promise – he can now marry Jean, at last. Rose Armiger, he says to Jean, 'has made us free'. Jean protests: 'It's her triumph – that our freedom is horrible!'[29] Tony has to agree. The two do not leave the stage, as it were, hand in hand when the curtain comes down on this almost tragic 'ugly duckling' of a novel. Begley uses the phrase 'ugly duckling anomaly' in his introduction to distinguish this from other novels by James: in this one, the vulnerable innocent is 'murdered in the absolute physical sense'.[30] (The 'anomaly' is, I would say, that this ugly duckling has no chance of becoming a swan.) Edel calls it 'the story of a brutal crime'. Both Begley and Edel see the murder as somehow governing and clouding the whole.

The crime is indeed horrible, but I've come to believe that it is incidental, conceivably inevitable given Mrs Bream's dying wish. James sees 'a precedent' that has nothing to do with the child's murder but everything to do with a web of relations that are child-like in their aggressions and suppressions and exaggerations and blamings. Right from the start, with that extracted promise, based on her own unhappy relation to her stepmother, Mrs Bream is not the adult in the room, but a silly girl projecting her childhood woes on the future of her child. And perhaps she sees in her all-too-likeable husband a lack of discernment? In any case, she sets in motion an easy plot, 'a divine little light to walk by', a gratification after all those years of failure on the stage, a way forward into the 'abysses' that Tony Bream, for a moment, allows himself to acknowledge, that Begley in his introduction calls 'the overpowering force and ignominy of the sexual drive'.[31] There's the 'precedent' James retrospectively appreciates. And what follows in these pages are thoughts about those and other 'abysses' in *The Awkward Age*, *The Sacred Fount*, *The Wings of the Dove*, *The Ambassadors*, *The Golden Bowl* and *The Sense of the Past*.

Henry James and the Great Tradition

I propose to bring together 'The Question of Our Speech', a lecture James delivered to the undergraduates of Bryn Mawr College on 8 June 1905, and the novel in which he makes the question of speech most explicit and problematic. But first I should try to clarify the portentous word 'tradition'. Starting with a few references.

In 1945 Wallace Stevens wrote a poem called 'Recitation after Dinner', later called 'Tradition'; in neither version was it published in his lifetime. In the poem, he considers various forms that tradition might be deemed to take – such as experience, memory or law –

but in the end he settles for the form given to us in the *Aeneid*:

> This is the form
> Tradition wears, the clear, the single form,
> The solid shape, Aeneas seen, perhaps,
> By Nicholas Poussin, yet nevertheless
> A tall figure upright in a giant's air.

Stevens says of this figure that

> The father keeps on living in the son, the world
> Of the father keeps on living in the world
> Of the son.

Finally, he says of these keepings that they are

> Survivals of a god that we have loved.[1]

In the issue of *Poetry* magazine for December 1913, Ezra Pound wrote a brief note on 'the tradition', as he called it. 'The tradition,' he said, 'is a beauty which we preserve and not a set of fetters to bind us.'[2] That is an honorific description, but

Pound also used the word without the honour, as in later references to 'the fustian tradition' and the tradition of *The Yellow Book*. A tradition could apparently be any value or system of values that draws attention to itself as an entity, a prejudice, a custom or an action. In 'The Question of Our Speech' James refers to 'truths of tradition, of aspiration, of discipline, of training consecrated by experience' and later to 'our admirable English tradition'.[3] These are tributes, but not definitions or even descriptions.

When Eliot published 'Tradition and the Individual Talent' in the *Egoist* of September 1919, he restored the honour without clearly identifying its recipient. The essay, despite its title, has little to say about tradition, once it has warned that if you want to be traditional you must start by having the historical sense and exerting it. In its few pages, Eliot's essay is rather a poetics in brief: it speaks of poetry, the poet and Eliot's insistence that the poet has 'not a "personality" to express, but a particular medium, which is only a medium and not a personality, in which impressions and experiences combine in peculiar and unexpected ways'. He then quotes a passage he much admired in *The Revenger's Tragedy* and finds in it 'an intense attraction towards beauty and an equally intense fascination by the ugliness which is contrasted with it and which destroys it'.[4] It is not clear that this combination of subtle and conflicting feelings has anything to do with tradition. Eliot says, in effect, that if you want such complex feelings, you must surrender yourself 'to something which is more valuable'.[5] He does not say what that more valuable thing is: it may be something in another poem, the bias of a language, the force of a genre or certain social practices such as good manners. It may be anything that asserts itself as more valuable than the bravado of the individual talent, the writer's private mind.

This marks the first difference between Eliot and James. James does not admit that the individual talent should suppress itself in favour of any other force. Social chance gave him most of his themes, but when he had handed over one of them to his mind, that organ – as he called it – took full responsibility for its conduct. In his preface to *The Awkward Age* he writes:

The truth is that what a happy thought has to give depends immensely on the general turn of the mind capable of it, and on the fact that its loyal entertainer, cultivating fondly its possible relations and extensions, the bright efflorescence latent in it, but having to take other things in their order too, is terribly at the mercy of his mind.

That organ has only to exhale, in its degree, a fostering tropic air in order to produce complications almost beyond reckoning.[6]

Such would be the freedom a novelist would enjoy, subject only to the nicety of the formal kind to be accomplished. James's prefaces are elaborate accounts of the freedom he practised and the obstacles he had to meet.

Eliot returned to the theme of tradition in 1933 when he gave the Page-Barbour lectures at the University of Virginia, lectures which are more bad-tempered than they have any good reason to be. They make tolerable sense only if we suppose that a nation ideally consists of many villages, each of them inhabited by the same kind of people, comfortably enough off not to want to pack their little bags and go somewhere else. In the first lecture, Eliot brought forward two capitalized words, Tradition and Orthodoxy, partly to distinguish them and partly to show a relation between them. 'I hold,' he said, 'that a tradition is rather a way of feeling and acting which characterizes a group throughout generations; and that it must largely be, or that many of the elements in it must be, unconscious; whereas the maintenance of orthodoxy is a matter which calls for the exercise of all our conscious intelligence.' Further:

> The two will therefore considerably complement each other. Not only is it possible to conceive of a tradition being definitely bad; a good tradition might, in changing circumstances, become out of date. Tradition has not the means to criticize itself; it may perpetuate much that is trivial or of transient significance as well as what is vital and permanent. And while tradition, being a matter of good habits, is necessarily real only in

a social group, orthodoxy exists whether
realized in anyone's thought or not.[7]

Tradition, in Eliot's usage, is a force that deserves
at least that we pay attention to it. We may criticize it, since it can't criticize itself. Orthodoxy is
his euphemistic word for Christianity. The notion
of tradition in relation to 'the social group' was
the source of much of the trouble that Eliot
brought upon himself in those lectures: if the
group is to persist as a group, it must exclude
those who do not belong to it by race or family.

F.R. Leavis was the critic who paid the most
sustained attention to tradition as Eliot invoked it.
He worried the term in several numbers of his
magazine *Scrutiny* and again in the first chapter of
The Great Tradition, published in 1948. That book
has been immensely influential, beginning with
the new generation of students who, having survived the war, went to university and took up
English studies. Leavis was their master, though a
few of them remained with him long enough to
revile him. He was much indebted to Eliot, to
begin with, but he deplored Eliot's conversion to

the Anglican Church in 1927. I think that Leavis's concern with tradition was an attempt to establish the moral seriousness of English studies while having nothing – at least nothing explicit – to do with religion. Matthew Arnold made that position feasible by maintaining that poetry could take the place of religion. Santayana rattled some cages by proclaiming that 'religion and poetry are identical in essence, and differ merely in the way in which they are attached to practical affairs. Poetry is called religion when it intervenes in life, and religion, when it merely supervenes upon life, is seen to be nothing but poetry.'[8]

If you agreed with Arnold or Santayana, you would hold that fiction could take the place of a dogmatic morality by presenting life as a riot of quandaries, each to be resolved in a community. Leavis's practice was to find the great tradition of English fiction in the few writers in whom he decided that it was manifest, and to make the values of the tradition emerge from a close reading of their novels. The great tradition, he declared, was embodied in certain novels by Jane Austen, George Eliot, Henry James, Joseph

Conrad, and D.H. Lawrence. 'It is in terms of
the major novelists, those significant in the way
suggested, that tradition, in any serious sense,
has its significance.'[9] In *The Great Tradition* he
concentrated on George Eliot, James and
Conrad. For various reasons, he left Jane Austen
in the capable hands of his wife, Q.D. Leavis,
and the critic and psychologist D.W. Harding.
He postponed the major consideration of
Lawrence till time permitted a book on him,
which he published in 1955. That left dangling,
in *The Great Tradition*, the questions of Dickens
and of Emily Brontë. There was a time when
Leavis regarded Dickens as merely a great
entertainer, but by 1948 he had reformed his
mind, largely on the persuasion of Q.D. Leavis
and the appreciated strength of *Hard Times* and
Little Dorritt. Dickens needed a book to himself,
and got it in *Dickens the Novelist*, written in col-
laboration with Q.D. Leavis and published in
1970. As for Emily Brontë: in *The Great
Tradition*, Leavis excused himself from saying
anything about *Wuthering Heights* 'because that
astonishing work seems to me a kind of sport'.[10]

I think he means that it came from nothing and has led to little or nothing – it is a phenomenon, a remarkable lark, but it doesn't participate in the great tradition. I can't make any other sense of Leavis's commentary.

Leavis's feeling for tradition is entirely literary: it does not acknowledge any other element in the general culture, such as economics, politics or religion; it involves a correction of literary history, which he regards as critically null because indiscriminate. Tradition is the relation, critically ascertained, between what, in literature, comes before and what comes after, as Richardson and Fanny Burney make certain things possible for Jane Austen and therefore provide the lineaments of a tradition. Leavis's fundamental claim is that the writers he finds fulfilling the great tradition not only 'change the possibilities of the art for practitioners and readers' but are also 'significant in terms of the human awareness they promote; awareness of the possibilities of life'.[11] They are 'all distinguished by a vital capacity for experience, a kind of reverent openness before life, and a marked moral intensity'.[12] The word 'life' in these and many other sentences is made to do a lot of work, mainly work of exclusion. Leavis's sense of life was aggressively narrow; it rejected many experiences which another man or woman would regard as treasures. His values were those of the realistic novel, until Lawrence extended somewhat – but only somewhat – Leavis's understanding of realism.

Leavis accepts, mainly under the jurisdiction of Yvor Winters's *Maule's Curse*, that James was also a major figure in an American tradition: he was 'a product of the New England ethos in its last phase, when a habit of moral strenuousness remained after dogmatic Puritanism had evaporated and the vestigial moral code was evaporating too'.[13] But Leavis doesn't take those conditions, or even James's relation to Hawthorne, as removing him from the English tradition. James inhabits that tradition mainly because of his relation to Jane Austen and George Eliot, as evidenced particularly by the kinship between *The Portrait of a Lady* and the good part of *Daniel Deronda* that Leavis liked to call *Gwendolen Harleth*. 'Henry

James wouldn't have written *The Portrait of a Lady* if he hadn't read *Gwendolen Harleth*.'[14]

The chapter on James in *Maule's Curse* has been extended and clarified by Allen Tate's essay on Emily Dickinson in his *Reactionary Essays* and by R.P. Blackmur's gloss on that in one of his essays on James. I'll quote the gist of it from Blackmur:

> Emily Dickinson came exactly at the dying crisis of Puritan New England culture – not at the moment of death, but at the moment – it was years long – when the matrix began to be felt as broken. Spiritual meaning and psychic stability were no longer the unconscious look and deep gesture worn and rehearsed lifelong; they required the agony of doubt and the trial of deliberate expression in specifically, willfully objective form. Faith was sophisticated, freed, and terrified – but still lived; imagination had suddenly to do all the work of embodying faith formerly done by habit, and to embody it with the old machinery so far as it could be used. There was no

other machinery available. Thus the burden of poetry was put upon the New England version of the Christian sensibility.[15]

James faced much the same conditions, but he responded to them more affably: he felt no agony on that score. In *The American Scene* he writes of New England:

> Here was no church, to begin with; and the shrill effect of the New England meeting-house, in general, so merely continuous and congruous, as to type and tone, with the common objects about it, the single straight breath with which it seems to blow the ground clear of the seated solidity of religion, is an impression that responds to the renewed sight of one of these structures as promptly as the sharp ring to the pressure of the electric button.[16]

James chose not to be daunted by the hard words of religion. His mind lived without benefit of clergy, but it was generally decent in its secularism. When he had to speak the words of religion, he tended to look about to see whether there might not be other words in common usage which would do the work – for him, anyway – nearly as well. He provides an example of this 'translation downward' or debunking in his essay of 1910 called 'Is There a Life after Death?' where he replaces the religious word 'soul' by the secular word 'personality'. Even more daringly he replaces the word 'belief' by the common word 'desire'. He says that it is not a question of belief, a word he has not used in this essay,

> but of desire so confirmed, so thoroughly established and nourished, as to leave belief a comparatively irrelevant affair. There is one light moreover under which they come to the same thing—at least in presence of a question as insoluble as the one before us. If one acts from desire quite as one would from belief, it signifies little what name one gives to one's motive. By which term 'action' I mean action of the mind, I mean that I can encourage my consciousness to acquire that

interest, to live in that elasticity and that affluence, which affect me as symptomatic and auspicious. I can't do less if I desire, but I shouldn't be able to do more if I believed. Just so I shouldn't be able to do more than cultivate belief, and it's exactly to cultivation that I subject my hopeful sense of the auspicious; with such success—or at least with such intensity—as to give me the splendid illusion of doing something myself for my prospect, or at all events for my own possibility, of immortality.[17]

The 'splendid illusion' and 'my own possibility' are as far as James is prepared to go toward immortality. He can achieve it just as well by desire as by belief, or so he thinks, and desire has the great advantage that it does not call for any action as esoteric as belief; everybody knows what desire is. It has the further merit of being endlessly extensible; as Leo Bersani has noted, 'James is interested in desires freely improvised by intelligence'.[18] You could not improvise on belief while remaining serious. James's position in the essay is that, his consciousness being as endless as it seems to him, he can't conceive of its being brought to an end with the cessation of his body. What can he mean by immortality but fame, though he doesn't use the word? Tolstoy enjoys life after death because many people continue to read *Anna Karenina* and *War and Peace*. If James is so bold as to replace belief by desire, I would expect to find him replacing the imperatives of doctrine by the more agreeable laws of taste or decorum, to find sanctity replaced by tone, prayer by acts of consciousness.

There is another wild equation in *The Golden Bowl* when Fanny Assingham says to her husband 'I shall be as magnificent at least as I can' and the conversation takes off:

Bob Assingham got up. 'And you call *me* immoral?'

It made her hesitate a moment. 'I'll call you stupid if you prefer. But stupidity pushed to a certain point *is*, you know, immorality. Just so what is morality but high intelligence?'[19]

Saving one's soul would be replaced, for a Jamesian artist, by achieving form on particular occasions, as, in a community, it would be sufficiently achieved by finesse of speech. Addressing the Bryn Mawr students, James said that the question of communication was that of speech:

> All life therefore comes back to the question of our speech, the medium through which we communicate with each other; for all life comes back to the question of our relations with each other. These relations are made possible, are registered, are verily constituted, by our speech, and are successful (to repeat my word) in proportion as our speech is worthy of its great human and social function; is developed, delicate, flexible, rich—an adequate accomplished fact.[20]

James assumes that the women of Bryn Mawr will continue to speak English, but he fears that they will speak it wretchedly. Like the young people he heard speaking English, or what passed for English, during his long visit to America in

1904–5, they will probably slur their vowels, erase their consonants and say 'yeah' instead of 'yes'. That is: they will leave their civilization in the unachieved state in which they found it. I recall the passage in *The American Scene* where James, reflecting on the linguistic mishmash he heard on the streets of New York, says:

> The accent of the very ultimate future, in the States, may be destined to become the most beautiful on the globe and the very music of humanity (here the 'ethnic' synthesis shrouds itself thicker than ever); but whatever we shall know it for, certainly, we shall not know it for English—in any sense for which there is an existing literary measure.[21]

Leavis's *The Great Tradition* does not proceed in these terms. He is always in a hurry to enforce what he regards as the necessary discriminations of literary criticism. He does not show you what it is like to read any of the great novels. When he quotes a passage, it is invariably as evidence of the critical discrimination he has already arrived at. Some of his comments are designed to bring any discussion of the relevant question to an end. When he says that he finds *The Ambassadors* 'boring', he leaves nothing further to be said, even by those, including myself, who don't find it boring. In the section on James in *The Great Tradition* and the essay on the later James in *The Common Pursuit*, Leavis gives himself space mainly to pronounce, and what he pronounces is that James is a great novelist on the strength of *Roderick Hudson* (whatever its faults), *The Europeans*, *The Portrait of a Lady*, *The Bostonians*, *Washington Square*, *The Awkward Age*, *What Maisie Knew* and several of the short stories. The best of the novels is *The Portrait of a Lady*, one of the greatest novels in the language. I quote a typical sentence to indicate the tone of Leavis's appreciation:

> What we have, for instance, in *The Europeans* and *The Portrait of a Lady* is a characteristic, (as I see it) critical and constructive interplay, done in dramatic terms, between different cultural traditions; an interplay in which

discriminations for and against are made in respect of both sides, American and European, and from which emerges the suggestion of an ideal positive that is neither.[22]

That sentence indicates a late stage in Leavis's reading of both novels: early stages are to be found elsewhere or to be taken for granted. Discrimination is the critical value to be enforced.

The most memorable aspect of *The Great Tradition* is Leavis's refusal to associate himself with a common understanding that the great James is to be found in his last three completed novels, *The Wings of the Dove* (1902), *The Ambassadors* (1903) and *The Golden Bowl* (1905). Taking his bearings and his vocabulary this time not from Eliot but from Pound's essay on James in the *Little Review* of 1918, Leavis found *The Wings of the Dove* 'fussily vague and intolerably sentimental'. Milly Theale, he says, 'for all the elaboration of indirectnesses with which James sets about generating her, remains an empty excuse for unctuous sentimentality. Kate Croy continues to engage more of our sympathy than suits the author's purpose.'[23] *The Golden Bowl* provokes Leavis to an extended paragraph:

> What we are not reconciled to by any aware-
> ness of intentions is the outraging of our
> moral sense by the handling of the adultery
> theme—the triangle, or rather quadrilateral,
> of personal relations. We remain convinced
> that when an author, whatever symbolism he
> intends, presents a drama of men and women,
> he is committed to dealing in terms of men
> and women, and mustn't ask us to acquiesce
> in valuations that contradict our profoundest
> ethical sensibility. If, of course, he can work a
> revolutionary change in that sensibility, well
> and good, but who will contend that James's
> art in those late novels has that power? In *The
> Golden Bowl* we continue to find our moral
> sense outraged.[24]

Leavis's appeal to 'our' moral sense is factitious. He suggests that we are all endowed with the same sense by nature (or at least that we all bow to his royal 'we'), and therefore that it can be relied upon, assuming that it is accompanied by sufficient intelligence, to enforce the same shared judgements on particular acts of conduct. He appears to be saying, without quite saying, that Maggie should have divorced the Prince, her father should have divorced Charlotte, and the four of them should have gone their separate ways for a while; presumably the Prince and Charlotte would marry, after a decent interval, and put up with their penury. But Leavis does not allow for another reading – in Blackmur's terms – that Maggie's recreation of her adulterous marriage, far from being an act of renunciation or disillusion, is 'an act of life fully realized and fully consented to, done because it is necessary to keep intact the conviction that life has values greater than any renunciation can give up or any treachery soil'.[25] Blackmur does not say what those greater values are, but he allows us to think that Maggie is in possession of them, or in possession of enough of them to redeem her marriage or at worst to make it feasible. I recall one of the essays in which James's father says that if husband or wife commits adultery, the partner should forgive and move on without vengeance or resentment to the next day.

The suggestion of an ideal positive that is neither European nor American is one of Leavis's perceptions, but he has not developed it. Any polarity that might be transcended would do well enough for James. I think of his recourse, so often and so vividly, to the comparative degree of the adjective, as if he could not be content with the positive degree of it that merely testifies to the condition of something's being what it is. No wonder he was alert to the Higher Law as Emerson and Thoreau invoked it, and to George Eliot's fondness for the comparative phrase 'a larger life' even though she doesn't allow Gwendolen to achieve it.[26] In *The Awkward Age* James has Mr Longdon wishing that Vanderbank had prepared him to defend himself, in an exchange with Mrs Brookenham, by bringing forward 'the art of conversation developed to the point at which it could thus sustain a lady in the upper air'.[27] Sometimes James can only make his peace with the future, which cannot be described but can be flung upon the present, as in the last sentence of his introduction to *The Tempest*, where he escapes from the disgust he feels for modern literary criticism by demanding something better and ascribing it to the future, its qualities being those of fencing: 'the finer weapon, the sharper point, the stronger arm, the more extended lunge'.[28]

Another example of James's preference for leaving his meaning dangle: near the end of *The Golden Bowl*, Maggie and the Prince are visited by Verver and his wife Charlotte. It is their last visit; the following day they are to set out for Southampton and American City. The four are at peace together, because they have decided to be at peace together. Maggie's is the presiding intelligence:

> To do such an hour justice would have been in some degree to question its grounds—which was why they remained in fine, the four of them, in the upper air, united through the firmest abstention from pressure. There was visibly no point at which, face to face, either Amerigo or Charlotte had pressed; and how

little she herself was in danger of doing so
Maggie scarce needed to remember.[29]

'In the upper air' has nothing to do with the sky.
It is a phrase almost without reference – nearly
free of it. It is a small version of the sublime,
which is where these four people have determined quietly to be while the visit lasts. I think
of calling James's style in this passage Free
Realism, which is Realism subject to the allowance he enjoys of escaping from its laws when he
chooses to sound a different tone. He was always
alive to the contingencies of life, and to Life as
the supreme value, but he allowed himself the
privilege of escaping its demands when he
needed to breathe in the upper air. In the introduction to *The Tempest* he says that Shakespeare
'sinks as deep as we like, but what he sinks into,
beyond all else, is the lucid stillness of his style'.[30]
That last phrase is nearly meaningless if we try to
think of it in any relation to Shakespeare. It is
not fanciful to suggest that James's style – or his
several styles – permitted him to diverge from
the accredited imperatives of a genre, if only to

enjoy a phrase or two of freedom. Some readers of James evidently think that his heart breathed only in the upper air; he was so hostile to the worldly institutions that he could not breathe for long in the air they secreted. I do in part agree with them, but I think his sentences, however cobwebby some of them are – this is Pound's adjective and Leavis's – keep him in the world and allow him only such vacations as he needs.

The Awkward Age (1899) is the novel in which James puts to the test his thoughts about speech and conversation. Mr and Mrs Edward Brookenham live in London, in a house in Buckingham Terrace. How they can afford this is a question. Edward has a sinecure that brings him in £1,400 a year, not enough to sustain wife, family and house. They have four children: a boy and a girl too young to count and the countable children Harold and Nanda. Harold is a no-good, a borrower of money he has no intention of repaying: his only asset is charm, mainly exercised on the frailties of women. Nanda is eighteen, therefore of marriageable age. Mrs B. leads a salon in which six or more friends drop in for tea and conversation. The main theme is how best to educate a girl – Nanda mainly – for marriage. Nanda is in love with Gustavus Vanderbank, the Adonis of the salon, but he is not in love with her; it is not clear that he even likes her. He is a senior civil servant with a decent salary but no spare money. It is a minor complication that Nanda's mother, Mrs B, is also in love with Vanderbank, or at least wants to take him as her lover if he were willing, which he appears not to be. Nanda has a friend, Aggie, of the same marriageable age. Aggie's aunt is the Duchess, widow of an Italian duke: she has taken Aggie to London, determined to find her a well-off husband, maybe in the salon. Some of the best conversations are disputes between the Duchess and Mrs B. The Duchess is rearing Aggie as a child and plans to keep her in that state of innocence. Mrs B has no plan for Nanda but she hopes that the world will not hurt her. There is no reason why it would.

Nanda is not a beauty, but she is distinctive. If Mrs B is to be believed, Nanda has a social conscience: at least, she occasionally brings her old nurse a pound of tea and, every Friday at three, she goes to read to the old women at the workhouse.

Not surprisingly, the salon disintegrates. Mrs Brookenham finds the conversations no longer interesting. Vanderbank drifts away, though Nanda tries to keep him close to her mother and makes him promise to do so, a promise he may or may not keep. The wealthy Mitchett marries Aggie, mainly because Nanda, with whom he is in love, urges him to marry her. He thinks that, in return, Nanda should give him unlimited social access to her. Mr Cashmore thinks he too is in love with Nanda, but he has no chance with her. A more formidable gentleman, Mr Longdon, elderly – more than fifty – has come up to London from his country house in Beccles, Surrey, to renew his ancient memories and see what the younglings are up to. In his youth he had been in love with Nandas's grandmother – Mrs B's mother – Lady Julia, but she married someone else. He is still enchanted with her.

When he first meets Nanda, in Vanderbank's flat, her resemblance to Lady Julia drives him beyond himself, and he rushes into another room to calm his nerves. Nanda soon follows, and they become not lovers but fast friends. On further experience Longdon decides that Nanda must be rescued from her mother. He tries to bribe Vanderbank to marry her by offering to endow Nanda with a large sum of money on their wedding day. Money is money, but Vanderbank declines. After a decent interval, Longdon invites Nanda to leave her parents in Buckingham Crescent and come to live with him. There is no question of marriage. He gives her a kiss on the forehead, she gives him one on the cheek. But there will be agreeable conversations in Beccles.

(I don't understand how Leavis's ethical sensibility was not outraged by this arrangement. Presumably the whole novel is a satire not against marriage as such but against marriages that are achieved by money and other conventional means, such that James's fiercest satirical thrust is not to have marriage at all. Friendship is better. Even better if there is also money.)

I have remarked that the conversations in the salon, while the going is good, are brilliant, but that is an evasive word. 'Intelligent' would be a nobler term of praise. Sometimes a sentence opens a dangerous field of implication and leaves it to the other speakers to take advantage of its risks or not. Vanderbank often makes statements so comprehensive that they should not be made at all, like this one to Nanda about Mr Longdon:

> 'I want you to do with me exactly as you do with him.'

Nanda doesn't answer, as she might: 'But what do you mean by "do"?' What we read is:

> 'Ah, that's soon said!' the girl replied in a peculiar tone. 'How do you mean, to "do"?'

We can't know what is peculiar in the tone of Nanda's reply, 'Ah, that's soon said'.[31] Vanderbank answers:

> 'Well then, to *be*. What shall I say?' Vanderbank pleasantly wondered while his foot kept up its motion. 'To feel.'

It's not clear whether his change of verb from *to do* to *to be* and then further to *to feel* is a translation of the first to be helpful or an escape from it to larger affiliations. It takes us a while to deduce from the little sequence that Vanderbank is merely saying 'If Mr Longdon lets you smoke, so will I'. This conversation between Nanda and Vanderbank at Mertie – Book Fifth, 'The Duchess' – could be played as an erotic game: if it were a scene in a play, the actor playing Vanderbank would do a lot with his eyes, his dangling foot, the degree of emphasis on certain syllables; the actress playing Nanda would either follow or lead and decide on her own form of play.

By my count, there are three narrators or narrative voices in this novel. As it happens, the three are heard in Book Fifth, 'The Duchess', in the scene at Mertle. The Duchess asks Longdon to talk to Aggie while she, the Duchess, finds a letter she wants to show to Lord Petherton. We are not given much of the conversation between Longdon and Aggie. Instead, Narrator A has a few sentences about Longdon:

A person who knew him well would, if present at the scene, have found occasion in it to be freshly aware that he was in his quiet way master of two distinct kinds of urbanity, the kind that added to distance and the kind that diminished it.

Interesting but not remarkable. At this point, by my reading, Narrator A hands over to the second narrator, whom I have been calling HJ:

Little Aggie differed from any young person he had ever met in that she had been deliberately prepared for consumption and in that furthermore the gentleness of her spirit had immensely helped the preparation. Nanda, beside her, was a northern savage, and the reason was partly that the elements of that young lady's nature were already, were publicly, were almost indecorously active. They were practically there for good or for ill; experience was still to come and what they might work out to still a mystery; but the sum would get itself done with the figures now on the slate.

We can almost feel HJ coming to the end of his resources, as the third voice, whom I call Henry James, takes over:

> Both the girls struck him as lambs with the great shambles of life in their future; but while one, with its neck in a pink ribbon, had no consciousness but that of being fed from the hand with the small sweet biscuit of unobjectionable knowledge, the other struggled with instincts and forebodings, with the suspicion of its doom and the far-borne scent, in the flowery fields, of blood.[32]

Pure Henry James: only he could have written that extraordinary sentence ending with 'blood'. Only he would have postponed that finality by inserting the aery phrase 'in the flowery fields'. The whole soliloquy is assigned to Longdon – 'Both the girls struck him' – but Longdon could not have been struck by what follows. He is intelligent up to a point, but beyond that point his mind is a courteous blank. Henry James has to take over.

Hesitant before calling *The Awkward Age* a great novel, and then deciding not to, I find provocation in one of Blackmur's passages, where he has examined two of James's short stories, 'The Figure in the Carpet' and 'Maud-Evelyn', before finding the same issue in *The Awkward Age*:

> In *The Awkward Age* the primary question is, what will happen to the publicly exposed relations of a set of people when the daughter of the house comes of social age and first takes part in those public relations? It is sometimes said that the relative failure of this book comes about because James restricted his presentation of his answer to a masterly use of scene and dialogue. But that argument would reduce Congreve to the stature of Wilde. The true cause of failure would seem to lie in the inability of all the characters in the book, including its presumably fresh and plastic young heroine, to bring into the conventions to which they restrict themselves the actual emotions and stresses that the conventions are meant to

control, but of which they were never, in a
living society, meant to be the equivalent.[33]

Blackmur's first sentence is not true: he is taking
James's preface at its word for the novel James
thought he had written rather than the one he
wrote. In the preface James speaks of 'the difference made in certain friendly houses and for
certain flourishing mothers by the sometimes
dreaded, often delayed, but never fully arrested
coming to the forefront of some value slip of a
daughter'. He means the difference it would
make to a salon of adults, women and men, when
Nanda would sit among them. Would the conversation take particular account of her innocence and edit itself in her favour? Or ignore
her? Good questions, but they do not occur in
the novel. James does not show Nanda sitting
among a circle of seniors. She has an important
conversation with her mother, privately, when
she comes back from a visit, with Longdon, to
the South Kensington Museum. Her final conversations with Vanderbank, Cashmore, Mitchett
and Longdon are also, with each, separate and

private. Nanda spends little time at home, till the end, when Mrs B calls her in, after she has spent about five months with Longdon in Beccles. At home, she reverts to her own room, upstairs, and receives her friends there. Not in the salon.

Blackmur's sentence beginning 'The true cause of failure' is hard to make sense of. I'll try to translate it. It seems to mean – seems, I could be wrong – that the characters talk endlessly about marriage but don't bring into their talk the independent force of marriage as an institution out there in the world. After the talk, there is only more talk. Blackmur holds, as most critics do, that good as words are, at least in principle, they should eventually yield privilege to what they refer to. Say what you like about marriage, you should acknowledge that out there in the world people are marrying and not just saying a few words. They are indeed saying a few words, at the behest of priest or minister or presider, but the words are a promise, an undertaking. The words yield to their meaning. In this respect Jane Austen's *Emma* is exemplary. There is not much talk about marriage: there is no need, because everyone knows that a marriage is, for the two people involved and for the society at large, the most far-reaching act of their lives. The whole novel deals with the mistakes Emma makes – her matchmaking mistakes, and the crucial insult she gives poor Miss Bates – and the hard lessons Emma learns from them, until the last pages when she becomes worthy to marry Knightley. Like the other marriages in the village, this one will take place in the local Protestant church, minister and congregation in attendance.

But this is not true of *The Awkward Age*. Some of the best passages in the book – the first argument between Mrs B and the Duchess, for instance – are about the best way to prepare one's daughter for marriage. There is only one new marriage in the book, that between Aggie and Mitchy. Mitchy marries her for a deplorable reason; she marries him presumably because her mother told her to say yes. The marriage has consequences, but they are conjectural: we are not invited to take much interest in them. There is only one old marriage that concerns us, that of the Brookinghams. However, we are led to believe, taking Nanda's word for it, that Edward would not care much even if Mrs B took Vanderbank as her lover. The idea that marriage is a sacrament does not occur to anyone.

The eighth book, 'Tishy Grendon', is the most intense because it is the book in which Mrs B decides to bring the salon to an end in a blaze of travesty. The scene is a dinner party at Tishy's. Vanderbank is the first to arrive, but he finds Nanda already there; she is lodging with Tishy for the time being. When Harold Brookingham arrives, Vanderbank greets him with a remarkable outburst of tastelessness: 'And here's Harold, precisely, as clear and crisp and undefiled as a fresh five-pound note'. Everyone in the room knows that Harold lives by pocketing any money he finds on his mother's coffee table, or in her purse, or in the wallet of anyone who can be the victim of a spurious loan. But Harold has the better part of this exchange – his charm wins the day.

Almost everyone is there: Tishy but not her estranged husband, Harry, who is yachting somewhere; Mr and Mrs B, Harold, Nanda, Longdon, Vanderbank, Mitchy, Aggie, Lady Fanny and Cashmore. The mayhem begins after dinner, in the upper rooms. Mrs B approaches Longdon and asks him, 'Why do you hate me so?' Vanderbank immediately intervenes to tell Longdon that he need not answer such a question.

> I should warn you, sir … that we don't con-sider that—in Buckingham Crescent cer-tainly—a fair question. It isn't playing the game—it's hitting below the belt. We hate and we love—the latter especially—but to tell each other why is to break that little tacit rule of finding out for ourselves which is the delight of our lives and the source of our tri-umphs. You can say, you know, if you like, but you're not obliged.[34]

Longdon doesn't respond to any of this. Meanwhile, Mrs B engages in fragments of des-ultory conversation until Tishy is referred to and then Mrs B says, 'her gloom, as you call it, is merely her broken nose'. Evidently Mrs B has already decided that her salon is finished and she might as well mark its end with force: 'The spell's broken; the harp has lost a string. We're not the same thing.' Vanderbank agrees: 'We used all to march abreast, but we're falling to pieces.' Vanderbank blames Mitchy, or rather his marriage, and Mrs B agrees. In the event, what Mrs B wants to say to Longdon is that, after having Nanda as company for five months, he must send her home. And, in the spirit of falling to pieces, she says so at last. As it happens, Edward Brookingham joins the group at this stage, and the Duchess asks him, '*Do* you, dear, want Nanda back from Mr. Longdon?' His reply is amazing: 'Want her, Jane? We wouldn't *take* her.' If this is a joke, it is so heavy that Mrs B must intervene to take the harm out if it. Which she does by saying that Edward and she dressed in a hurry and didn't have time 'for the usual rehearsal'.

> Edward, when we dine out, generally brings three pocket-handkerchiefs and six jokes. I leave the management of the handkerchiefs

> to his own taste, but we mostly try together in advance to arrange a career for other things. It's some charming light thing of my own that's supposed to give him the sign.[35]

A page or two of similar banter follow until Tishy remarks that Aggie and Pemberton are playing in the other room. Playing what, hide and seek? Tishy reports that Aggie has hidden a book and Pemberton is trying to find it. Maybe Aggie is sitting on it. Mitchett is thrown into gloom by these proceedings, even when Pemberton runs from the room, bearing in triumph the sought-after book, a questionable French novel on which Nanda has handwritten the name, Vanderbank, of its supposed owner. (This is the moment at which the novel gratifies the interest of Queer Studies. Nanda's handwriting on the book cannot protest when 'hand', cause of the romp between Pemberton and Aggie, is transposed by scholarly desire into 'fist', instrument of anal practice.) The evening is brought to an end when Longdon, who has had enough of it, says 'Good-night' to Tishy.

If, after reading this novel, we go back to James's Bryn Mawr lecture, we find that he is concerned with securing the nicety of English diction. He seems to think that if young women regularly say 'yes' and 'no', they will school themselves to larger observances. He doesn't raise the question 'what then shall we talk about?' He might have adverted to several issues: marriage, no marriage, love, sex, family, class society, politics, empire, law, race, democracy, religion, death, life after death. None of these was mentioned. He might also have held that it wouldn't matter what the students talked about, provided they allowed for the reply, 'Yes, but what do you mean by so-and-so?' – a scruple upon which *The Awkward Age*, as we have seen, depends.

What difference does it make that a novelist is deemed to participate with his or her fiction in a great tradition? What does it entail? My own notion is that a tradition is often well on its way to being a constituent of a culture. If a culture is then part of a nation, the tradition enhances it. If a particular tradition is meretricious, it should probably fall away, to be preserved if at all by antiquarians. Leavis's *The Great Tradition* is an act of cultural and therefore of social and political significance: it gave English readers something they did not know they had. They knew they had lots of novels, but he said: 'No, some of those works of fiction are far more valuable than the rest. They are to be treasured as we treasure Shakespeare's plays and Turner's paintings.' If England has a great tradition, in fiction, it means more than that the country has a flag, a national anthem and some majestic buildings – more because the literature has a critical relation to the values that are otherwise merely celebrated.

The Sacred Fount

I

On 3 December 1964 Hugh Kenner wrote to his closest literary friend, Guy Davenport, a letter that included the following:

> Query, was it [Henry] James who invented the point-of-view as *character*? Not as in Robinson Crusoe or David Copperfield, the first-person protagonist, but a kind of invisible inflection of the narrative, as in Fordie's Good Sojer [Ford Madox Ford's *The Good Soldier*]. Having just asked this question of myself for the 1st time, I hesitate to reread acres of fiction to settle it, and wonder if you've already an opinion. I am

trying to formulate what it was James *did* invent; X-ray should surely disclose something more skeletal than his pretzel-bending with the English sentence.[1]

Davenport replied at once, on 7 December, but not quite to the point, making several independent observations:

Point of view as character? [Henry] James, for my money, is the first man to tell an arch story. The *meaning* of the nuvvle is in us, if we got the point. He merely hints and suggests and feeds details ... Perhaps he refined irony as far as it has been refined. There are things that cannot be said. Such as what a James character feels ... A fog in Smollett is to hold up the villain or hero; a fog in James is like the fog in Prufrock. ... The twentieth century has grown carefully and logically into the architectonic. Which, of course, has always been there. The Iliad flows, scene after scene, a tight narrative; but all is as geometric as the vases of the period ... James is the earliest novelist to perceive that the architectonic design can be uppermost. (*The Sacred Fount* the extreme pure example; *Golden Bowl* his full-scale example.)[2]

In *The Pound Era* (1961) Kenner contrived his own answer to the question:

> James's effort to articulate such matters within the shape of the formal English sentence yielded the famous late style, where subject and verb are 'there' but don't carry the burden of what is said. Other syntactic structures do that.[3]

Those structures are subordinate clauses, I assume. Parentheses, sometimes.

At a dinner party in London on Sunday, 18 February 1894, Stopford Brooke gave Henry James two 'little ideas' for stories. The first came to nothing, but James made a note of the second:

> The notion of the young man who marries an older woman and who has the effect on her

of making her younger and still younger, while he himself becomes her age. When he reaches the age that *she* was (on their marriage), she has gone back to the age *he* was. Mightn't this be altered (perhaps) to the idea of cleverness and stupidity? A clever woman marries a deadly dull man, and loses and loses her wit as he shows more and more.

Or the idea of the *liaison*, suspected but of which there is no proof but this transfusion of some idiosyncrasy of one party to the being of the other—this exchange or conversion? The fact, the secret, of the *liaison* might be revealed in that way. The two things—the two elements—beauty and 'mind,' might be correspondingly, concomitantly exhibited as in the history of two related couples—with the opposition, in each case, that would help the thing to be dramatic.[4]

Nearly five years later, James reminded himself of the idea, with a difference:

Don't lose sight of the little *concetto* of the note in former vol. that begins with fancy of the young man who marries an old woman and becomes old while she becomes young. Keep my play on idea: the *liaison* that betrays itself by the transfer of qualities—qualities to be determined—from one to the other of the parties to it. They exchange. I see 2 couples. One is married—this is the *old-young* pair. I watch their process, and it gives me my light for the spectacle of the other (covert, obscure, unavowed) pair who are *not* married.[5]

James thought of the 'little *concetto*' as the makings of a short story, but as he started dictating it, it expanded; two couples could not be treated as briskly as one. Almost before he knew what he was doing, he had a novel on his hands, but without quite disposing of it as the shadow of a short story. Reluctance to waste his sentences, if nothing else, kept him going.

The Sacred Fount was published on 6 February 1901 in the United States and nine days later in England. James sent a few copies to friends, with little enthusiasm. Later, he excluded it from the New York edition of the novels and tales. When Mrs Humphry Ward wrote him an appreciative letter about the novel, he with some embarrassment removed the praise:

It was a remarkably accidental [book], and the merest of *jeux d'esprit*. You will say that one mustn't write accidental books, or must take the consequences when one does. Well, I do take them—I resign myself to the figure the thing makes as a mere tormenting trifle. The subject was a small fantasticality which (as I *have* to write 'short stories' when I can) I had intended to treat in the compass of a single magazine installment—a matter of eight or ten thousand words. But it *gave* more, before I knew it; before I knew it had grown to 25,000 and was still but a third developed. And then … I couldn't afford to sacrifice it; my hand-to-mouth economy condemned me to put it through in order not to have wasted the time already spent. So, only, it was that I hatingly finished it, trying only to make it—the one thing it *could* be—a *consistent*.

Few readers in James's vicinity saw the joke; it remains invisible to me:

Alas, for a joke it appears to have been, round about me here, taken rather seriously. It's doubtless very disgraceful, but it's the last I shall ever make! Let me say for it, however, that it has, I assure you, and applied quite rigorously and constructively, I believe, its own little law of composition.[6]

To James, 'accidental' meant, I think, that the idea was suggested to him by someone else and that it seemed a good idea at the time and occasionally thereafter but would not have the authority of his own invention. The 'little law of composition' has proved just as hard to see as the joke.

It was scarcely necessary for Stopford Brooke to give James the little *concetto*. If – an improbable if – I were invited to Newmarch as an unaccompanied guest, I might, strolling the gardens and with nothing pressing on my mind, wonder how those two, he and she, or he and he, or she and she, came together for conversation in that remote corner and what they found to engage each other for more than a desultory minute or two. My interest in such a question might start vague, with an air of innocence, but it might, with nothing much to distract it, concentrate itself to a sordid degree of prurience, at which point I hope I would desist and turn my mind in a healthier direction. James, dining out, welcomed hints of a story, but only small hints: he didn't want to know how the anecdote ended; he wanted to hold possible developments of it for himself.

The Sacred Fount is the only full-scale novel in which James used the 'first-person singular' as narrator. He thought the device fine for short stories and wrote many of them in that confidence. *The Aspern Papers* went as far with the device as he thought he should push it. In the preface to *The Ambassadors* he glanced at the possibility that he might have made Strether the narrator:

Had I, meanwhile, made him at once hero and historian, endowed him with the romantic privilege of the 'first person'—the darkest abyss of romance this, inveterately, when enjoyed on the grand scale—variety, and many other queer matters as well, might have been smuggled in by a back door. Suffice it, to be brief, that the first person, in the long piece, is a form foredoomed to looseness, and that looseness, never much my affair, had never been so little so as on this particular occasion.

'The long piece' was the novel. *Gil Blas* and *David Copperfield* might be thought to thrive on 'the double privilege of subject and object', as James calls first-person narrative, but this privilege is no good if the novelist wants to make 'certain precious discriminations':

Strether, on the other hand, encaged and provided for as *The Ambassadors* encages and provides, has to keep in view proprieties much stiffer and more salutary than any our straight and credulous gape [is] likely to bring home to him, has exhibitional conditions to meet, in a word, that forbid the terrible *fluidity* of self-revelation.[7]

In formal autobiography, James appears to be saying, anything goes. If some passages are extravagant, well, the extravagance can be taken as a further quality of the authoritative self. It can't be vetoed. Yeats and James, in their autobiographical books, say whatever they want to say, bring forward their choice themes, without worrying much about the terrible fluidity of their sentences. Poems and novels have stricter laws.

James uses the phrase 'the sacred fount' four times in this novel, where it appears to mean every force we have not asked of; it is impersonal, indeed aboriginal, it lies in wait. We cannot ask for it unless we are eligible to receive its gift. If we receive it, it transforms our life for good. Guy Brissenden is in love with his wife; he didn't ask to be, but he is – or rather, there it is. Grace Brissenden gets younger as she ages; she has had to extract new blood, time and bloom, from someone, 'and from whom could she so conveniently extract them as from Guy himself ... and he, on his side, to supply her, has had to tap the sacred fount: But the sacred fount is like the greedy man's description of the turkey as an "awkward" dinner dish. It may be sometimes too much for a single share, but it's not enough to go round.'

Much later, in the great Chapter 8, the narrator asks May Server what has happened to her. There is no reply, nor does he mention the sacred fount, but the word 'passion' seems to stand for the fount in its consuming force: 'I saw as I had never seen before what consuming passion can make of the marked mortal on whom, with fixed beak and claws, it has settled as on a prey.'[8]

II

The Sacred Fount begins as if it were to be a social novel much like any other. There is to be an August weekend party at Newmarch, a large country house with lavish gardens, reachable by train from Paddington about an hour out on the Birmingham line. It is an upperclass party, of course. Three guests have arrived early at the station.

One, the narrator, is alone, apparently a middle-aged bachelor given no name or further characterization, so we may as well call him N for short. He recognizes a fellow guest, Gilbert Long, a coxcomb whom he has no desire to travel with, 'so I looked for a seat that wouldn't make us neighbors'. The plan fails, and he finds Long 'come down to me as if for a greeting'. At the end of a minute 'we were talking together quite as with the tradition of prompt intimacy'. Long goes to find a porter and comes back also with a lady unknown to N. When the three are settling themselves in N's carriage, the lady rebukes him: 'I don't think it very nice of you not to speak to me.' At last and mainly by her voice, N recognizes her as Grace Brissenden. So the three of them are together, and they have the carriage to themselves. At first they talk, but as the train gathers speed, they give up trying to compete with its music. 'Meanwhile, however, we had exchanged with each other a fact or two to turn over in silence.' The fact or two include these. Grace's husband, Guy, is to come to Newmarch by a later train and to bring on Lady John, a fact that when mentioned by Grace causes Gilbert Long to express some interest and surprise. 'Didn't you really know?' Grace asked him with a smile. Know what or how much? Then there is the question of Long himself. How has he, whom N recalls as a bore, turned into a delightful companion, easy in talk and manners? Before the train started, Long went out on the platform to buy a newspaper, and N seized the minute to put a question to Mrs Brissenden and got an abrupt answer: 'A very clever woman has for some time past—' and N completes her sentence, 'Taken a particular interest in him?' Lady John perhaps? If the generous woman-in-question is Lady John, she must have enough wit for two. Mrs Brissenden is herself a quandary. It is common knowledge that she married a notably good-looking man more than ten years her junior. She is perhaps forty-two or forty-three, he is not yet in his thirties, but she – whom N recalls as plain if not ugly – is now pretty and might be twenty-five. What is going on? N has evidently a harsh notion of marriage: spouses can't be equal – one of them has to be superior and to win. For the moment, N must content himself with the reflection that to each of his companions 'something unprecedented had happened'.

Arrived at Newmarch, N mingles and after a while meets the few guests who seem to matter: Ford Obert, a portrait painter, the only guest who has a profession or appears to need one; Lady John, who disappoints N because imagination in her presence 'was but the weak wing of the insect that bumps against the glass'; Mrs Server, charming as ever, though Obert tells N that 'she's too beastly unhappy'; and Guy Brissenden, the young husband who looks old, any age, he could be sixty or more – 'Nothing could have been stranger than the way that, fatigued, fixed, settled, he seemed to have piled up the years':

It was as if he had discovered some miraculous short cut to the common doom. ...

It took me but a minute then to add him to my little gallery—the small collection, I mean, represented by his wife and by Gilbert Long, as well as in some degree doubtless also by Lady John: the museum of those who put to me with such intensity the question of what had happened to them.[8]

'Happen' is one of two words in this novel that carry more than their normal weight: the other is 'matter', as in 'What is the matter with Grace?' In *The Sacred Fount* to happen is to occur without apparent cause, though a plausible cause may later be proposed; it has also a suggestion of the definitive – if something has happened, many other possibilities can be counted out to make space for that one. In N's view, to happen is to participate in the theory he is beginning to formulate or the enigma that falls short of a theory. To happen is to come into being as with the force of destiny – it changes your life. If the happening is meritorious, it may be thought to have issued from the sacred fount, which is a store of whatever keeps the human world going. If not meritorious, it counts

as tragic. 'Matter' does not always point to a physical defect, a loud voice at table or a dress in bad
taste. In this novel the question might be prompted
by someone taking short steps, seeming to be suffused by an aura or walking the gardens alone.
Any sign would do. In Chapter 4, when Long
entertains Mrs Server so well, leaving the art
gallery, that she is convulsed with laughter, Obert
asks N: 'What's the matter with them?' There's
nothing the matter with them, unless Obert is
using the word in an occult sense. N uses it in a
standard sense when he finds himself becoming
anxious: that, then, is the matter with him. So he
answers Obert's question with a dash: 'The matter
with them? I don't know anything but that they're
young and handsome and happy – children, as
who should say, of the world; children of leisure
and pleasure and privilege.'[9]

That seems to be enough for the moment.
But James has N circumnavigating the word as if
he grieved to see it drift away into the company
of other less significant words. Near the end of
the book, Grace wants to cut the theme short,
but N doesn't:

'Does it particularly matter?' Mrs. Briss inquired. I felt my chin. 'That depends a little—doesn't it?—on what you mean by 'matter'. It matters for your meeting my curiosity, and that matters, in its turn, as we just arranged, for my releasing you. You may ask of course if my curiosity itself matters; but to that, fortunately, my reply can only be of the clearest. The satisfaction of my curiosity is the pacification of my mind.[10]

The *old–young* part of N's theory is simple, with the Brissendens as exemplars:

The particular case before us, I easily granted [to Obert] was a fair, though a gross, illustration of what almost always occurred when twenty and forty, when thirty and sixty, mated or mingled, lived together in intimacy. Intimacy of course had to be postulated. Then either the high number or the low always got the upper hand, and it was usually the high that succeeded.[11]

The sacred fount, to attempt a grander account, is the source or spring of life, youth, fire or whatever value is deemed absolute. To tap it is to draw what is needful, if all goes well. It goes well with Guy and Grace: he sacrifices for her his youth and beauty, takes on a slumped pair of shoulders and a withered back because he is passionately in love with her. But he knows he pays a price, and he consorts with May Server in shared woe until Grace puts a stop to it and brings husband home. The relation of Grace and Guy may be 'the relation of a fellowship in resistance to doom', but it does not resist every form of doom.

The second part of N's theory, the *liaison*, is more difficult. In Chapter 3 he tells Grace that Lady John can't be the inspiring woman in the case of Gilbert Long. Who then? As soon as Grace asks the question, she becomes N's confederate in the hunt. A little later Obert, too, becomes a minor confederate, to the extent of promising to keep his eyes open, but he imposes on himself and on N a restriction that would make all the difference if it were obeyed to the letter:

'We ought to remember,' I pursued, even at the risk of showing as too sententious, 'that success in such an inquiry may perhaps be more embarrassing than failure. To nose about for a relation that a lady has her reasons for keeping secret—'

'Is made not only quite inoffensive, I hold'— he immediately took me up—'but positively honourable, by being confined to psychologic evidence.'

I wondered a little. 'Honourable to whom?'

'Why, to the investigator. Resting on the *kind* of signs that the game takes account of when fairly played—resting on psychologic signs alone, it is a high application of intelligence. What's ignoble is the detective and the keyhole.'[12]

The *OED* defines psychologic as 'the practice of logical reasoning based on psychological observations and judgements rather than on abstract propositions'. Obert thinks of N's theory as a game with severe, gentlemanly rules. Refusing to play the detective, he welcomes the scientist. N thinks only of the hunt. But Obert's employment at the party doesn't last long. He loses interest in the game as soon as he has prescribed its rules. He doesn't want the game to have consequences. N's preoccupation is nobody's business. Meanwhile Mrs Brissenden has persuaded herself that Gilbert Long's muse is Mrs Server, and she ascribes N's sluggishness to his being in love with that lady himself: he will do anything to protect her from being found out.

This is one of several moments in the novel when James is thinking of the short story it might better have been. The first sentence of the book told us that there was to be 'a large party' at Newmarch, but we meet only three or four guests in addition to the three at Paddington. We do not have a sense of a crowd thronging the gardens or the rooms. This bears on a passage in R.P. Blackmur's essay on *The Sacred Fount*:

Thus we see that as novelist James is the hidden conscience of his characters, and as conscience he is himself their sacred fount. For is not conscience indeed that imaginative resource of which, if one has it at all, one has too much for a single share and yet not enough to go round?[13]

N should have enough conscience for the few characters he notices, but he hasn't. He is hostile to Lady John for no good reason. He tells us that she is stupid, her mind closed, but when he lets her speak she has formidable things to say. No one else thinks to accuse N, to his face, of having 'the imagination of atrocity' or to scold him for trying to be a providence. N has a decent answer, a silent one, the reflection that 'she could get so near without getting nearer', which proves to his satisfaction that he is more intelligent than any of his company, starting with Lady John. But she is right about his playing providence; he has broken Obert's rule that the confederates must stick to psychologic terms.

III

The Sacred Fount is the only novel by Henry James that I have read six times. My motive is impure. The book is not at all as powerful as *The Portrait of a Lady* or *The Wings of the Dove*, but I find myself hurrying to get to Chapter 8, which I hold to be a most gratifying piece of writing, unless a seventh reading changes my mind by reducing the pleasure. I concede that N is the dominant character in the book, because he has the privilege of the first person, but he is not as wise as he thinks he is, or as humane. He is like a diplomat who thinks he has the best cards in his hand and can't lose. Or the man in Marianne Moore's poem 'Marriage' who loves himself so much that he cannot admit a rival to that love.

Chapter 8 starts as a celebration, on N's part, of 'the beauty of having been right'. Every element seems to fit his theory. Newmarch's landscapes assent to his presence (the following paragraph has been quoted by other readers, but no matter):

There was a general shade in all the lower reaches—a fine clear dusk in garden and grove, a thin suffusion of twilight out of which the greater things, the high tree-tops and pinnacles, the long crests of motionless wood and chimnied roof, rose into golden air. The last calls of birds sounded extraordinarily loud; they were like the timed, serious splashes, in wide, still waters, of divers not expecting to rise again. I scarce know what odd consciousness I had of roaming at close of day in the grounds of some castle of enchantment. I had positively encountered nothing to compare with this since the days of fairy-tales and of childish imagination of the impossible. *Then* I used to circle round enchanted castles, for then I moved in a world in which the strange 'came true.' It was the coming true that was the proof of the enchantment, which, moreover, was naturally never so great as when such coming was, to such a degree and by the most romantic stroke of all, the fruit of one's own wizardry. I was positively—so had the wheel revolved—

proud of my work. I had thought it all out, and to have thought it was, wonderfully, to have brought it. Yet I recall how I even then knew on the spot that there was something supreme I should have failed to bring unless I had happened suddenly to become aware of the very presence of the haunting principle, as it were, of my thought. This was the light in which Mrs. Server, walking alone now, apparently, in the grey wood and pausing at sight of me, showed herself in her clear dress at the end of a vista. It was exactly as if she had been there by the operation of my intel- ligence, or even by that—in a still happier way—of my feeling.[14]

This passage asks to be interpreted with a certain allowance because every detail is offered as if it issued from N's wizardry. It won't do for a reader to say: 'I've never heard rooks shout like that.' The divers are, I hope, various kinds of water birds. They can't be sure of rising again because their instinct only counts for so much and the rest – the rising – has to be taken on trust. The simile is obscure, unless N takes the extraordinarily loud cawing of the rooks as meaning that they can't be sure of finding resting places at night.[15] But 'the operation of my intelligence' has first right, and 'my feeling' comes next and is still larger. We might call the whole passage 'subjective realism'.

For once, the sequence of N's experiences is edifying. It is as if he were to come out to the gardens with nothing on his mind but appreciation: the dusk, twilight, tree-tops and pinnacles, the woods, golden air, what the noisy rooks seemed to be like, some castle of enchantment, fairy-tales as in childhood not merely given but 'the fruit of one's own wizardry'. Finally and exultantly, 'the haunting principle, as it were, of my thought': the rhyme of 'thought' and 'brought', fulfilled by the presence of May Server pausing at the end of a vista. The insistence of 'exactly', bold against the admission of 'as if', testifies to the illusion and, at the same moment, to its right to be counted. The conceit by which Mrs Server seems to be there 'by the operation of my intelligence, or even by that— in a still happier way—of my feeling' is not ashamed of itself. In James's novels the women are examined more analytically than the men because they are deemed to be more highly developed. He reminded himself of this superiority in *The American Scene*:

> Nothing, meanwhile, is more concomitantly striking than the fact that the women, over the land—allowing for every element of exception—appear to be of a markedly finer texture than the men, and that one of the liveliest signs of this difference is precisely in their less narrowly specialized, their less commercialized, distinctly more generalized, physiognomic character.[16]

At any moment since the beginning of this chapter, N could speak love to Mrs Server, but he doesn't. He knows he is good for her, but only with the limitation of being second best. We are not told much about her distress. She has had three children and lost them. We hear nothing of a Mr Server. But we are free to apply to Mrs Server what N says to himself in her presence:

I saw as I had never seen before what consuming passion can make of the marked mortal on whom, with fixed beak and claws, it has settled as on a prey. She reminded me of a sponge wrung dry and with fine pores agape. Voided and scraped of everything, her shell was merely crushable. So it was brought home to me that the victim could be abased, and so it disengaged itself from these things that the abasement could be conscious. That was Mrs. Server's tragedy, that her consciousness survived—survived with a force that made it struggle and dissemble.[17]

Further, N being reluctant to leave the subject:

I saw how it was that whereas, in such cases in general, people might have given up much, the sort of person this poor lady was could only give up everything. She was the absolute wreck of her storm, accordingly, but to which the pale ghost of a special sensibility still clung, waving from the mast, with a bravery that went to the heart, the last tatter of its flag.[18]

If these sentiments, all N's, added together amount to love, they are still, to Mrs Server, the sentiments of her second best friend:

> I ended by divining that she had none the less her obscure vision of a still softer ease. Guy Brissenden had become in these few hours her positive need—a still greater need than I had lately amused myself with making out that he had found her. Each had, by their unprecedented plight, something for the other, some intimacy of unspeakable confidence, that no one else in the world could have for either. … Oh, how I made it out that if it was indeed very well for the poor lady to feel thus in *my* company that her burden was lifted, my company would be after all but a rough substitute for Guy's![19]

He imagines that Mrs Server, restored to speech, would say that Guy 'is as much better than you as you are than everyone else'.

The wonder of this chapter is the simultaneous presence of three needs: May Server's, Guy's and N's, not in competition but in doomed company. May Server's need is fulfilled because to have communed with Guy's is to experience fulfilment, if only while the circumstances last. Guy's need is assuaged, if only while Grace is absent and he is permitted to know what another relation, even if brought to a swift end, might have been like. N has the decency to withdraw, knowing that second best in need and love is good but not good enough.

After dinner at Newmarch there was a recital for guests in the drawing room, by 'an interesting pianist who had given a concert the night before at the near county town and been brought over during the day to dine and sleep'. If readers are content – as I am not – to identify N with the person and genius of Henry James, a few sentences of this Chapter 9 would make them pause and reflect with some unease on James's social, cultural and political conscience. I am not Terry Eagleton, nor was meant to be. When I attend a piano recital, I determine to listen to the music and, as far as possible, to postpone other considerations. They will – or may – insist later. Yeats wrote about the necessity of holding in a single thought reality and justice. Difficult, perhaps impossible. If anyone has discovered how to do it, I have not heard. For now, I think it enough that I quote the relevant sentences. N is still thinking of May Server and of the meeting he has had with her but not of that alone:

> What for my part, while I listened, I most made out was the beauty and the terror of conditions so highly organized that under their rule her small lonely fight with disintegration could go on without the betrayal of a gasp or a shriek, and with no worse tell-tale contortion of lip or brow than the vibration, on its golden stem, of that constantly renewed flower of amenity which my observation had so often and so mercilessly detached only to find again in its place. This flower nodded perceptibly enough in our deeply stirred air, but there was a peace, none the less, in feeling the spirit of the wearer to be temporarily at rest. There was for the time no gentleman on whom she need pounce, no lapse against

which she need guard, no presumption she
need create, nor any suspicion she need
destroy. In this pause in her career it came
over me that I should have liked to leave her;
it would have prepared for me the pleasant
afterconsciousness that I had seen her pass,
as I might say, in music out of sight.[20]

The 'constantly renewed flower' is N's image –
not necessarily James's – for the urbane, disinter-
ested recurrence of natural processes, indifferent
to our resolute ideologies of politics, religion or
other saving prejudices. We are not told what the
pianist played: no need. It is by music as such
that N can imagine that he may be at peace with
May Server and she with herself. Not a word
about the other marvel of civilized life, provided
by the gardeners, housekeepers, maids, footmen
who carry the suitcases, cleaners, cooks and other
servants who keep the affluence of fine things
flourishing.

The part of the book that James wrote so 'hatingly', to bring the tormenting thing to an end, is
not clear. I find no show of bad temper in his later

sentences. If we assume it's the last three chapters, we have to recall that some parts of N's theory have been verified. Gilbert Long remains transformed, partly on the evidence of the brilliant things he says – about the painting of the man with the mask – to Obert, an artist who should know such perceptions when he hears them.

When Grace keeps her appointment with N for their nocturnal meeting, she blurts out: 'It's nonsense. I've nothing to tell you. I feel there's nothing in it and I've given it up.' She has given up the conviction that Mrs Server must be the enabling woman. At this point, N divines, on no evidence clear to me, that Grace has Gilbert Long behind her, she is his emissary, and her denial of this is a lie: she denies that she has talked to anyone. In a long conversation – to call it that for the moment – Grace makes few statements. She tells N that he is crazy. She says that Lady John and Gilbert Long are indeed lovers, though Long remains the dope he always was. May Server tried to make up to Guy Brissenden, unsuccessfully, because Guy told Grace about it and Grace put a stop to it. Conversation is not the right word for these exchanges. The right word is eristic, a school of Greek philosophy which did not see itself as the pursuit of truth but as a battle of words in which the sole object was to win. Grace Brissenden has the last word, though she gets it 'with her negations arrayed and her insolence recaptured', also by two or three lies and by changing the subject to N's insanity. 'My poor dear, you *are* crazy, and I bid you good-night!' are her last words, but not N's:

Nothing but the sense of them—on my taking it from her without a sound and watching her, through the lighted rooms, retreat and disappear—was at first left me; but after a minute something else came, and I grew conscious that her verdict lingered. She had so had the last word that, to get out of its planted presence, I shook myself, as I had done before, from my thought. When once I had started to my room indeed—and to preparation for a livelier start as soon as the house should stir again—I almost breathlessly hurried. Such a last word—

the word that put me altogether nowhere—
was too unacceptable not to prescribe afresh
that prompt test of escape to other air for
which I had earlier in the evening seen so
much reason. I *should* certainly never again,
on the spot, quite hang together, even
though it wasn't really that I hadn't three
times her method. What I too fatally lacked
was her tone.[21]

The word 'tone', I need hardly say, comes from
music, where it refers to an ideal propriety in the
performance, say Brendel's Beethoven or Cortot's
Chopin. It then extended its aura to conversation, public behaviour, taste. If in conversation I
resent your tone or you resent mine, there is a
question of bad manners, perhaps sarcasm or
shrillness for which there is no decent reason.
The last sentence of N's reflection in the passage
just quoted is questionable. There is no evidence
that Grace's management of tone is better than
N's. On the contrary, to call him insincere or
crazy is a crude way out. N would not have
sought this midnight talk: Grace summoned

him, to make him accept that her husband was now securely back in her quarters, where he belonged. N wants to take the earliest train back to Paddington and to leave the eristic extravagance of Newmarch well behind him.

I have left Kenner's formula and Davenport's cadenza without comment. We need a passage demonstrably in the later style. This one will do, while N is enjoying the piano recital:

> We thought, accordingly, we continued to think, and I felt that, by the law of the occasion, there had as yet been for everyone no such sovereign warrant for an interest in the private affairs of everyone else. As a result of this influence, all that at dinner had begun to fade away from me came back with a rush and hovered there with a vividness. I followed many trains and put together many pieces; but perhaps what I most did was to render a fresh justice to the marvel of our civilised state. The perfection of that, enjoyed as we enjoyed it, all made a margin, a series of concentric circles of rose-colour (shimmering away into the

pleasant vague of everything else that didn't matter) for the so salient little figure of Mrs. Server, still the controlling image for me, the real principle of composition, in this affluence of fine things.[22]

Keeping, for economy, to the sentence after 'the marvel of our civilized state', I note that it is indeed a sentence, having a subject, a verb and several objects: the subject, 'The perfection of that'; the verb, 'all made'; the first of many objects, 'a margin'. Kenner's formula from *The Pound Era* is useful: subject and verb are there, necessarily, for formal reasons, but they do little of the expressive work. This would not be true in another style: 'Jesus wept.' In James's sentence the work of expression is done mainly by subordinate phrases that extend themselves by a principle of near-synonymity. The phrases are not identical, but they co-exist agreeably in N's mind. We are to accept without fuss the concentric circles of rose-colour, even if this is the only passage of English prose in which they are likely to appear. We are also to accept the destiny that James gives them in that ravishing parenthesis. One particular easily suggests another in this affluence of fine things.

I can't make much out of Davenport's claim that James is the first man to tell an arch story, unless he is using 'arch' as a Poundian short for architectonic. Again, the *OED* is not helpful. The *Yale Dictionary of Art and Artists* says that, when used in writings on art, 'architectonic' may mean that a painting or sculpture depicts architecture or is used in an architectural setting, but it may also signify architecture-like compositional stability and weight, a reliance on vertical and horizontal accents. Davenport also quotes from Paul Klee's diaries that a drawing is both architectonic – the rhythm the artist has given the surface – and descriptive. I can see that *The Sacred Fount* is layered, but that doesn't clarify its structure. But it is probably better to take Davenport's phrase – 'the first man to tell an arch story' – as what it appears to be, 'arch' as an adjective qualifying 'story'. The *OED* is not especially useful on 'arch' as an adjective. I find it better to go back to James's story 'Crapy Cornelia', a story I've looked at for other reasons, where the word is doing a lot of work. In the story, belatedly, White-Mason recognizes Mrs W's guest as Cornelia Rasch, an old friend in earlier New York. Her presence rejoices his sight and he exclaims: 'May I come and see you the very first thing?' A conventional answer might be 'Yes, I would be pleased to see you', but instead we read this:

> Indeed the supreme oddity was that the manner of her reply to his request for leave to call should have absolutely charmed his attention. She didn't look at him; she only, from under her frumpy, crapy, curiously exotic hat, and with her good little near-sighted insinuating glare, expressed to Mrs. Worthingham, while she answered him, wonderful arch things, the overdone things of a shy woman. 'Yes, you may call—but only when this dear lovely lady has done with you!' The moment after which she had gone.[23]

We are not told what the wonderful arch things were, except that in a different idiom they are the overdone things of a shy woman. 'Arch' then seems to mean odd, independent, not quite belonging to the genre in which it finds itself – hence in Davenport's Poundian flourish, 'the *meaning* of the nuvvle is in us, if we got the point: he merely hints and suggests and feeds details'. However: 'there are things that cannot be said. Such as what a James character feels.' Not quite true. We know what Mrs Server feels. And what N's two assistants feel when they give up and throw in their cards. And what N feels when he catches the earliest train back to Paddington.

I still think that a better analogy than architectonics – well-established, indeed – is painting. Reading one of James's later novels is like walking slowly through a gallery of modern art, paying gratified attention (if possible) to each painting. Many of the paintings disdain to be asked what does it mean while issuing a strong invitation to pay attention. When I come to Chapter 8, I am not ready to be ravished, as I am when I read 'Among School Children' and 'Ash Wednesday', but after a few sentences, I give in.

The Wings of the Dove

In his preface to *The Wings of the Dove* James does not say that his novel makes for difficult reading, but he says that it requires a reader to pay continuous attention, and he claims that the more the attention is needed, the richer the reward for giving it:

> Attention of perusal, I thus confess by the way, is what I at every point, as well as here, invoke and take for granted; a truth I avail myself of this occasion to note once for all—in the interest of that variety of ideal reigning, I gather, in the connexion. The enjoyment of a work of art, the acceptance of an

irresistible illusion, constituting, to my sense, our highest experience of 'luxury,' the luxury is not greatest, by my consequent measure, when the work asks for as little attention as possible. It is greatest, it is delightfully, divinely great, when we feel the surface, like the thick ice of the skater's pond, bear without cracking the strongest pressure we throw upon it.[1]

James's ideal reader, it is clear from this, belongs to that 'eventual sublime consensus of the educated' which he invoked in the preface to 'Lady Barbarina'.[2] Only an alert reader could rise to James's occasions. He is not writing for lazy consumers or for common members of the broad-backed public. James does not claim that his ideally qualified and alert reader would find nothing in the book to complain of. He confesses to defects and limitations more widely, by my count, than in any other preface. He admits that he didn't do enough with Lionel Croy to maintain a sense of his dreadful impingement, throughout the story, on his daughter Kate:

The image of her so compromised and compromising father was all effectively to have pervaded her life, was in a certain particular way to have tampered with her spring; by which I mean that the shame and the irritation and the depression, the general poisonous influence of him, were to have been shown, with truth beyond the compass even of one's most emphasized 'word of honour' for it, to do these things.

But where do we find him, at this time of day, save in a beggarly scene or two which scarce arrives at the dignity of functional reference?[3]

James might also have confessed – but he didn't – that he took too much for granted with Milly Theale. A young American princess with wealth and a terminal disease is likely to be a moving presence, but James doesn't make her live – while the going is briefly good – as fully as he thinks. He knows that it is by the act of living that even the 'sickest of the sick' is appealing, but he hasn't gone far enough with that knowledge. His presentation of Milly frustrates our desire to know her. He gives us little to know; she disappears into the symbol that represents her – the dove is the only form in which she may be said to live. Because she coincides with her symbol, there is nothing further for her to be. That is why it makes no difference, either to Kate or to us, whether Densher is in love with Milly before or after her death or in love with his memory of her: these are one and the same. James concedes that he didn't make enough of Densher or of Mrs Lowder or Susan Stringham, or of every fruitful ramification he merely sketched in the chapters set in Venice. He failed to adjudicate, as justly as he wanted to, between the claims of 'picture' and of 'drama', as he called his choice values. He notes that the second half of the novel is skimped and is therefore bristling with 'dodges … for disguising the reduced scale of the exhibition'.[4]

James also raises a delicate question about his treatment of the main characters, whom he thinks of as centres of consciousness: has he forfeited the advantage of keeping each of them distinct from the others, at least long enough to establish a 'post of observation' and something worth observing? Or has he allowed one centre of consciousness to melt into another? On the whole, he seems to think himself justified in having settled for a practical 'fusion of consciousness'[5] in the early presentation of Kate and Densher, because of their 'subjective community'.[6] The same consideration is supposed to hold for the later occasions on which Milly and Susan share a 'more or less associated consciousness'.[7] James is sanguine, too, about his having Densher's 'direct vision of the scene at Lancaster Gate' replaced by Kate's 'apprehension, her contributive assimilation, of his experience', presumably because Kate's vision is the one that counts.[8] But he doesn't raise a far more difficult question: to what extent is the narrator allowed to assimilate to himself the several centres of consciousness, such that they exist only in a subservient relation to his?

Leo Bersani has argued, in response to this question, that while James is committed in principle to present his fiction through centres of consciousness, he has not offered to efface the narrator from this novel. In fact, the narrator not only takes command of the administration of the story, but often speaks for particular characters as if they could not speak up fully for themselves. In many passages it is impossible to say where the particular centre of consciousness is operative, where it is silenced and where the narrator moves to the front of the stage, addressing the audience directly. One of Bersani's instances is in the second volume, book six, when for the first time Densher visits Milly alone in her hotel in Brook Street. Densher finds her notably tender to him, from the sympathetic consideration apparently that his feelings for Kate are not reciprocated: he is interesting, to begin with, because he is unhappy, and he is unhappy, supposedly, because he has spent in vain his passion for Kate. Kate has left Milly in no doubt about the wastage and that she does not intend to respond to Densher. Densher should, as a gentleman, set Milly straight and tell her the truth, that Kate and he are in love, but he settles for the conclusion that anything he can think of doing would be just as

gross as his doing nothing. He is loath to interfere with the 'pure pleasure' that Milly evidently
takes in liking him.[9] In any case, Kate has apparently left Milly free to do whatever she wants
with Densher:

> What Milly 'liked' was to do, it thus appeared,
> as she was doing: our young man's glimpse of
> which was just what would have been for
> him not less a glimpse of the brutality of
> shaking her off. The choice exhaled its shy
> fragrance of heroism, for it was not aided by
> any question of parting with Kate. She would
> be charming to Kate as well as to Kate's
> adorer; she would incur whatever pain could
> dwell for her in the sight – should she con-
> tinue to be exposed to the sight – of the
> adorer thrown with the adored. It wouldn't
> really have taken much more to make him
> wonder if he hadn't before him one of those
> rare cases of exaltation – food for fiction,
> food for poetry – in which a man's fortune
> with the woman who doesn't care for him is
> positively promoted by the woman who does.

It was as if Milly had said to herself: 'Well, he can at least meet her in my society, if that's anything to him; so that my line can only be to make my society attractive.' She certainly couldn't have made a different impression if she had so reasoned.[10]

It is not clear in this passage, as Bersani notes, 'just how far Densher's thoughts go' and where the narrator takes over:

First of all, James states as potential what the reader knows has been a real thought in Densher. He writes that Densher's awareness that Milly is doing what she most wants to be doing was 'what would have been for him' a glimpse of the brutality of chucking her. We know by this time in the novel that Densher considers that it would be indelicate to spoil the 'pure pleasure' Milly takes in pitying him, and what he sees at this moment works in his mind, whether or not he makes the conscious connection, to reinforce his decision to keep the truth from her. James is perhaps filling in what Densher doesn't have time for. But it is also characteristic of James to include several potential thoughts in his record of a character's state of mind. And here a possible observation in Densher becomes a real element in the narrator's point of view on the scene.[11]

There is, I think, a little more. 'It thus appeared': to whom? 'Our young man's glimpse' separates the narrator from Densher, but 'what would have been' has the narrator experiencing for Densher if not speaking for him: he does this by indicating what would have been the reasonable thing for Densher to feel. The sentence about the choice – Milly's – is the narrator's report. So is the next one, except that it is in the 'indirect free style' according to which the ostensibly third-person narrator uses the words the character – Milly – would use if she were conducting the narrative. Milly would say – or words to this effect – 'there is no reason why I should not be as charming to Densher as to Kate, whatever pain I feel when I see him adoring her'. 'It wouldn't really have taken much more to make him wonder': is that what Densher is thinking about himself – is he wondering about 'one of those rare cases of exaltation'? Unlikely. Or is this what he might have wondered if he had the narrator's qualities in addition to his own? 'It was as if …' Again, to whom does this seem to be the case? Is Densher imagining what Milly is thinking to justify the special treatment she is giving him? Or is the narrator imagining Milly's thinking these thoughts as the kind of thoughts such a woman would think to justify her actions? 'She certainly couldn't have made a different impression if she had so reasoned.' Did she so reason or not? An impression on whom? On Densher? On herself? On anyone who happened to be 'in the know'? He doesn't advert to the fact – Bersani's point – that the narrator has insisted on seeing everyone's experience with his own eyes. James is concerned with having the relevant perceptions expressed, without troubling himself to show at every point whose perceptions they are. That is one of the felicities available to omniscient narration or to first-person narration when it claims the privilege of knowing everything that needs to be known.

In the preface, James seems to feel rueful about having 'scarce availed myself of the privilege of seeing with Densher's eyes'[12] and having, instead, seen with Kate's, but the consequence of Bersani's argument is that *The Wings of the Dove* becomes not entirely the novel James thought it was but an allegory in the guise of a novel. It is a first-person narrative in which the characters – each distinct up to a point and separate enough for an ostensibly realistic novel of manners – become functions of the narrator's mind, possible choices within that entity, 'alternatives of [his] inner allegiance'.[13] 'It is the inner allegiances that count, not social behavior.'[14] James reconciles – though Bersani doesn't say this – the sordid intrigue of Kate and Densher with the high talk that surrounds it by having every action in the novel transformed into a possibility the narrator sees. The narrator freely entertains what the characters are permitted to do because the several things they do are equally possibilities of his thinking – that is, of virtual behaviour –

among which he sends his mind moving. It is the movement that counts. The characters are not eliminated, and we are free to judge what they do, but each plays his part within a dance of hypotheses – in other words within an allegory, a tableau of gestures. As Bersani puts it:

> [Densher] is the self examining its possibilities. Kate is the way of power, acquisition, an active reaching out for the world. Milly, on the other hand, is the image of the self giving itself to the world, taking nothing. Each character is shown choosing the role he or she will take in the principal moral drama of the novel, which begins with Kate's encouraging Densher to cultivate Milly.[15]

Furthermore, even when the characters are used as centres of consciousness, the issues among them remain the same, as Bersani notes:

> Not only do the language and style of the various parts of the novel point to a single perspective from which character and

situation are seen throughout the book; the specific moral issues are the same for the three main reflectors. We have the same inner drama in all three cases, with, of course, the important difference of opposite final choices. Indeed, James's main reflectors in the novel are different images of the passive but highly responsive self trying to find its way in a maze of demands being made on it by the external social world. Kate is oppressed in Book One by the insistent claims of her father, her sister, and her aunt; Milly feels the pressure of what she believes is everyone's benevolence; and Densher is painfully aware that his future with Kate depends on his acquiescing in the demands she and Mrs. Lowder are making on him.[16]

Not all of these exertions of pressure have the same force. The pressure on Kate is the most extreme – she hasn't enough money: 'the hard fluent fact in which modern society has its being', as Lionel Trilling described money.[17] Money is obdurate against her determination to rise in the world, if only because it sets the whole drama in motion: there would have been no story – or a different one – if Kate had been well off and married a duke. But the exertions of pressure on the main characters are all constituents of the narrator's experience within the allegory he sets going. The diction in the minds of the main characters – allusions to doves, wings, lionesses, panthers and princesses – is like the images in a play of Shakespeare's: pervasive but not intuited equally by every character. Shakespeare has imposed the images, such that they govern the atmosphere and tone of the play, even while he gives every character the freedom of being who and what he or she is, subject to the allegorical design of the whole.

There is further evidence that *The Wings of the Dove* did not turn out as James intended. He wanted it to be Milly's story, but it turned out to be Densher's. In the preface he says:

> The idea, reduced to its essence, is that of a young person conscious of a great capacity for life, but early stricken and doomed,

condemned to die under short respite, while
also enamoured of the world; aware moreover of the condemnation and passionately
desiring to 'put in' before extinction as many
of the finer vibrations as possible, and so
achieve, however briefly and brokenly, the
sense of having lived.[18]

But that is not the image we have of Milly. Her
'great capacity for life' is not shown. She sails
from New York, crossing the Atlantic without a
word of observation, and in Switzerland she
takes a walk one afternoon in the Alps. In
London she makes a visit to the National Gallery,
and in Venice she gives a party for Sir Luke
Strett and his niece and appears in white to distinguish the occasion, but for the rest she receives
guests, goes to a few dinner parties in London
during the season and takes the first opportunity
of falling in love. She tells Susan that she wants
abysses,[19] but these are concentrated into the
single abyss of love. The 'great capacity for life' is
seen far more strongly in Kate than in Milly, not
because Kate devours every experience she can

find – she goes to the National Gallery but not to see the pictures – but because we feel her will bodied forth against the conditions it has to meet. She lives because she is determined to win her life, by whatever device she can use.

When I say that Milly's story has been largely displaced by Densher's, I mean that the drama of the book consists in the action of forces that point him toward the conscience he has not yet acquired. Will he assent to the force of conscience, which his experience with Milly may or may not establish? If he does, what will the consequence be for his relation to Kate? Will his example transform her to the point of their having an acute conscience in common? Or will she remain what she has always been, a young woman trying to bend the hard conditions of her life to her desire? If this reading is at all just, then Milly becomes – until the end – the frail, shadowy but beautiful presence to which the worldly forces refer. Densher becomes what we are told he sees himself as being, on his return from Venice to the London of Lancaster Gate:

He himself for that matter took in the scene again at moments as from the page of a book. He saw a young man far off and in a relation inconceivable, saw him hushed, passive, staying his breath, but half understanding, yet dimly conscious of something immense and holding himself painfully together not to lose it. The young man at these moments so seen was too distant and too strange for the right identity; and yet, outside, afterwards, it was his own face Densher had known. He had known then at the same time what the young man had been conscious of, and he was to measure after that, day by day, how little he had lost.[20]

Otherwise put: how much he had got away with, how grandly Milly in Venice had let him off. We are to believe 'that something had happened to him too beautiful and too sacred to describe'. So no attempt is made to describe it, except to say 'how little he had lost' in the event. 'He had been, to his recovered sense, forgiven, dedicated, blessed; but this he couldn't coherently express.'

Except to bring those three large past participles to bear on the experience, whatever it had been otherwise and in addition.

This passage brings up a difficulty for the reader of *The Wings of the Dove*. Indeed, it suggests that we are dealing with two categories of difficulty. In the first, we have to deal with blanks, parts of the novel in which we are not told what we would reasonably have expected to learn. In the second, we are dealing with redundancies, where we are given more than we asked for – more than we could have felt the need of – and get no help in making sense of it. Each of these categories makes a difficulty for the reader, but in each it is a different difficulty. In the first, we have to leap over the vacancy and wonder, if we reach the far side, what it was we leaped over. In the second, we have to haggle over what we are given and hope to rub away its obtrusiveness or otherwise wrestle it to the ground. In the first, if we interpret the vacancy according to our best plan, we are trusting ourselves to arbitrariness: we make whatever shift we can to fill it, but we suspect that any other device would have done just as well. In the second, we do the best we can to interpret the hard detail in relation to whatever we have up to that point decided. Either way, we make our interpretive zeal carry us across the vacancy or around the crux. I'll mention a few instances of each category, starting with blanks.

We are never told what's wrong with Lionel Croy. Is he a charming wastrel, or has he done something further to wreck his wife and children? James concedes that he should have kept up the wretchedness of it throughout the book, if only to give Kate every incentive to make herself rich and independent. Near the beginning, Kate tells Densher that her father 'has done some particular thing. It's known—only, thank God, not to us. But it has been the end of him.'[21] But even much later, when Densher goes to Kate at her sister's house, we are specifically not told what Lionel did that was so dreadful. He is in bed, but not ill. Kate shakes her head: 'Father's never ill. He's a marvel. He's only—endless.' When did he come to Marian's house? 'Three days ago—after he hadn't been near her for more than a year, after he had apparently, and not regrettably, ceased to remember her existence; and in a state which made it impossible not to take him in.' Was he in want? 'No, not of food, of necessary things—not even, so far as his appearance went, of money. He looked as wonderful as ever. But he was—well, in terror.' In terror of what? 'I don't know. Of somebody—of something. He wants, he says, to be quiet. But his quietness is awful.' What does he do? 'He cries.'

What has he done? 'If you love me—now—don't ask me about father.'[22]

> The intention announced in it he should but too probably know; only that would have been, but for the depths of his spirit, the least part of it. The part of it missed forever was the turn she would have given her act.[23]

If it is audible to the spiritual rather than to the sensual ear, it is like the 'ditties of no tone' addressed to the same transcendent faculty in Keats's 'Ode on a Grecian Urn'. We can believe that Densher hears this faint far wail from Venice only if we immensely add to the signs of an achieved conscience we have been waiting for him to show. He is dealing with his own blank, the unread letter, and we have to decide to what extent his imagination has indeed extraordinarily filled out and refined the missing turn of Milly's act. In the nature of the case, this is more than we should be asked to do: whatever he does and whatever his imagination does by way of filling out and refining, he cannot divine the turn 'she would have given her act'. Nor can we. At best, he has a revelation in which not enough is revealed – the rest is by definition blank and must be left in that state. Kate threw the letter into the fire because she knew what it contained – the commercial gist of it, which is the only part of it she was interested in. She was indifferent to the particular turn of Milly's act, that being a secret she was willing (either for conscientiousness or hauteur) to leave between Milly and Densher. But in fact Densher lets Kate burn Milly's letter because he doesn't want to know the turns of phrase and style it contains. He wants to replace the letter by the thought of it, treasuring the wonder without the constraint of knowing precisely what it is. He wants a relation to the letter other than the limiting one of knowledge. He has replaced Milly, too, by the thought of her, a thought that includes his no longer loving Kate:

> The thought was all his own, and his intimate companion was the last person he might have shared it with. He kept it back like a favourite pang: left it behind him, so to say, when he went out, but coming home again the sooner for the certainty of finding it there. Then he took it out of its sacred corner and its soft wrappings; he undid them one by one, handling them, handling it, as a father, baffled and tender, might handle a maimed child. But so it was before him—in his dread of who else might see it.[24]

So he guards this relic of the princess. The sacred radiance of it is such that we are deemed not to want to know the force of his love, now that Milly is dead. That knowledge, too, disappears in the temple he has built to worship her.

One word may be taken to represent these blanks, the word 'everything'. It is used in the book with strange reiteration. When Densher asks Kate what her father has done, she answers that 'he has done everything' and Densher cogently says: 'Oh—everything! Everything's nothing.'[25] When Susan asks Milly is she in trouble, in pain, Milly answers:

> 'Not the least little bit. But I sometimes wonder—!'

> 'Yes'—she pressed: 'wonder what?'

> 'Well, if I shall have much of it.'

> Mrs. Stringham stared. 'Much of what? Not of pain?'

> 'Of everything. Of everything I have.'

> Anxiously again, tenderly, our friend cast about. 'You "have" everything: so that when you say "much" of it—'

'I only mean,' the girl broke in, 'shall I have it for long? That is if I have got it.'

She had at present the effect, a little, of confounding, or at least of perplexing her comrade, who was touched, who was always touched, by something helpless in her grace and abrupt in her turns, and yet actually half made out in her a sort of mocking light.

'If you've got an ailment?'

'If I've got everything,' Milly laughed.

A moment or two later, when Susan says, 'Tell me, for God's sake, if you're in distress,' Milly answers, 'I don't think I've really *everything*.'[26]

Clearly, or obscurely, the word 'everything' here is like 'x' in algebra, meaningless until you put other signs in relation to it. We may believe in the mocking light, but we can't know what it's directed upon. At the beginning, Susan seems to think 'everything' means money, youth, all the gifts, but when Milly starts talking again about 'everything', Susan has no idea what she means, except that, whatever it is, Milly must be assumed to have it. At the end of the conversation, Milly seems not to be listening to Susan; it is as if she were talking to herself about the 'everything' she may or may not comprehend. Readers are in much the same state of bewilderment as Susan is: no amount of haggling can make any difference or fill the vacancy.

Sometimes, 'everything' is stabilized by the 'nothing' that accompanies it, as when Kate turns Densher's question about Milly – 'making nothing of the fact that I love another?' – into 'making everything; to console you'.[27] Or it is filled out by its relation to 'anything'. At Matcham, when Lord Mark gathers that Milly is seriously ill and asks her: 'And you don't do anything?' she answers: 'I do everything. Everything's this … I'm doing it now. One can't do more than live.' 'I shan't have missed everything,' she continues, and Lord Mark says, 'Why should you have missed anything?'[28] Sometimes, 'everything' gets enough precision – or at least enough suggestiveness – from the limited 'it' that incites an amplifying response. When Kate tells Densher that she doesn't see any particular significance in Lord Mark's spending Christmas with Mrs Lowder – 'that's all I see in it' – he picks up on the 'it' and expands it to a tribute, though a qualified one: "'You see in everything, and you always did," Densher returned, "something that, while I'm with you at least, I always take from you as the truth itself.'"[29] The assertiveness of 'everything' and the repeated 'always' are emptied of much of their value by the qualification 'while I'm with you at least': the comprehensiveness of these terms is shown up as specious – they are already void. But in some cases the claim of 'everything' is made with a challenge to the one who hears it: he is to fill it to whatever amount he decides it holds and to run the risk of falling short, to his embarrassment. After the crisis in Venice, Susan comes to visit Densher and to have her knowledge of the crisis completed. She claims to know a lot about it, but not everything: 'No—not everything. That's why I've come.'[30] Obviously, Densher is not willing to tell her that he and Kate have made love in that very room. After more conversation, Susan implores him to give Milly a denial that what Lord Mark has said is true. He asks: 'But a denial … of exactly what?' He hopes that she will narrow the range of it, but in fact she enlarges it: 'Of everything,' she answers; and the narrator tells us that 'everything had never even yet seemed to him so incalculably much'. "Oh!" he simply moaned into the gloom.'[31] In this case Densher knows what 'everything' means, but Susan doesn't. She is willing to take his solemn word for it, if only he will give it, but he doesn't.

The redundancies present another form of difficulty, since they seem to say that they could be resolved by readers sufficiently intelligent and alert, while the blanks remain incorrigible, whatever intelligence is brought to bear on them. In the first volume, book three, Milly goes out by herself for a walk up in the Alpine meadows and brings with her a Tauchnitz book she apparently hasn't begun to read. After a while, Susan follows her and finds the book on a rock: soon afterwards, she sees Milly sitting near the edge of a cliff. Susan is anxious – she even thinks it possible that Milly might be contemplating suicide; but she puts aside that idea and, without approaching Milly, turns back toward the inn. When she comes again to the rock where the Tauchnitz book is lying, Susan scribbles on the cover 'à bientôt' and continues on. After an hour or two, Milly returns. Now the incident has its purpose. It impels Susan to decide that Milly will not commit suicide: on the contrary, she will take 'full in the face the whole assault of life, to the general muster of which indeed her face might have been directly presented as she sat there on the rock'.[32] Well and good. But we don't know what Milly has been thinking. We have no reason to credit what Susan concludes that she has been thinking (despite James's confidence, in the preface, that he was justified in handing over to Susan the privilege of divining Milly's thoughts). The sole force of Susan's speculations, in this Alpine scene, is that no other speculations are offered. But what is the point of the Tauchnitz book and of the little message that Susan scrawls on its cover? When Milly comes back to the inn, she hasn't the book with her – it is still lying on the rock – and she gives no sign that she has read the message. The episode is never mentioned again.

There are other redundancies, or at least equivocations. In the conversation between Susan and Densher, after the crisis in Venice, Susan says that Lord Mark, thinking to improve his chances with Milly by incriminating Kate and Densher, is 'an idiot of idiots'. 'And he's thought so awfully clever,' Densher says. The conversation continues with Susan saying:

'So awfully—it's Maud Lowder's own view. And he was nice, in London,' said Mrs. Stringham, 'to me. One could almost pity him—he has had such a good conscience.'

'That's exactly the inevitable ass.'

'Yes, but it wasn't—I could see from the only few things she first told me—that he meant her the least harm. He intended none whatever.'

'That's always the ass at his worst,' Densher returned.[33]

We're clearly meant to take this as formidable, if not decisive, though it's not clear why the possession of a good conscience – and the wish to do no harm – are the typical attributes of an ass. Would the opposite disposition be morally better? Densher evidently thinks he is leading the discussion along more subtle lines than those normally to be expected from Susan, but twenty-five pages later, when Densher is telling Kate about his days with Sir Luke in Venice and Kate is asking him how he knows that Sir Luke brought Milly back to life, Densher says:

'I see. I feel. I was with him again as I had been before—'

'Oh and you pleased him too? That was it?'

'He understood,' said Densher.

'But understood what?'

He waited a moment. 'That I had meant awfully well.'

'Ah, and made *her* understand? I see,' she went on as he said nothing.[34]

'That I had meant awfully well' is, as Bersani says, 'shockingly inadequate as justification of [Densher's] failure to take any active steps to save Milly. But in terms of the allegorical level of the drama, this integrity of inner intention is wholly sufficient to redeem his early temptation to choose the alternative of being Kate offered him.'[35] The moral question appears not to matter, since the only thing that matters is the co-presence of such several motives as possibilities – no more than possibilities – in the narrator's mind. But we can hardly be supposed to have forgotten the earlier conversation between Densher and Susan in which Lord Mark's having meant awfully well is not allowed to count for anything but a sign of his being an idiot.

A further redundancy occurs in the second volume, book seven, after Sir Luke's interview with Susan and Susan's meeting with Kate. Milly knows that Susan must now mostly pity her, and that she in turn and for that reason must pity her:

Ruefully asking herself on what basis of ease, with the drop of their barrier, they were to find themselves together, she felt the question met with a relief that was almost joy. The basis, the inevitable basis, was that she was going to be sorry for Susie, who, to all appearance, had been condemned in so much more uncomfortable a manner to be sorry for her. Mrs. Stringham's sorrow would hurt Mrs. Stringham, but how could her own ever hurt? She had, the poor girl, at all events, on the spot, five minutes of exaltation in which she turned the tables on her friend with a pass of the hand, a gesture of an energy that made a wind in the air. 'Kate knew,' she asked, 'that you were full of Sir Luke Strett?'

'She spoke of nothing, but she was gentle and nice; she seemed to want to help me through.' Which the good lady had no sooner said, however, than she almost tragically gasped at herself. She glared at Milly with a pretended pluck. 'What I mean is that she saw one had been taken up with something. When I say she knows I should say she's a person who guesses.' And her grimace was also, on its side, heroic. 'But *she* doesn't matter, Milly.'

The girl felt she by this time could face anything. 'Nobody matters, Susie. Nobody.' Which her next words, however, rather contradicted. 'Did he take it ill that I wasn't here to see him?'[36]

Those words don't contradict what Milly has just said, or take the harm out of it. They acknowledge that other people – or at least a few of them – have feelings and are entitled to them. But the assertion that 'nobody matters, Susie. Nobody' is too comprehensive to be set aside; it stays in the air between Milly and Susan and can't be removed. If these words were spoken by Milly to herself, they might be condoned as meaning that, in the light of eternity, the death of one wealthy American woman can't be reckoned a catastrophe. But they are spoken to include the person to whom they are addressed. The enormity of them might be mitigated if they were taken to mean 'None of the people we have recently been thrown into association with, here in London, matters much to us—to you and me—in the end: we will live our destiny together'. But that interpretation is stretching things.

Another instance of redundancy is Milly's action in making Densher rich anyway, despite what he has done. There are hard choices of interpretation. Either it is a supreme act of grace, transcendently right, what a princess who is often deemed analogous to Christ or the Blessed Virgin would do if she were to fulfil her intention without being deflected. She acts from what T.S. Eliot in his major essay on Dante calls 'the higher dream' and we may think of Kate's as the lowest dream, except for the need that drove her to it and kept her there. Or it is a quiet act of revenge, as if she knew that the relation between

Densher and Kate could not survive the Christmas letter. R.P. Blackmur speaks of 'the permanent accursed gift of the strength of her forgiveness'.[37]

The title of the novel does not suggest revenge. Psalm 55.6 reads: 'And I said, Oh that I had wings like a dove! For then would I fly away, and be at rest.' That doesn't sound much like Milly. Psalm 68.13 has: 'Though ye have lien among the pots, yet shall ye be as the wings of a dove covered with silver, and her feathers with yellow gold.' On the last pages of the book, Densher and Kate take over the situation. He is resolute on having nothing to do with Milly's bequest. 'Your desire is to escape everything?' Kate asks, and Densher answers: 'Everything.' But Kate thinks to take up the old metaphor of the dove and to see her and Densher alike as together covered by its wings: 'I used to call her, in my stupidity – for want of anything better – a dove. Well she stretched out her wings, and it was to that they reached. They cover us.' Densher agrees, but the final test Kate imposes on him breaks them apart: that he will give his word of honour that he is not in love with Milly's memory. This resolves the question of their marriage; it is impossible. 'We shall never be again as we were!'[38] But it doesn't clear up the question of the accursed letter. James could not have allowed Milly, this heiress of the ages, to be defeated, even by an early death. But he could have suffused her forgiveness – as indistinguishable in its effects from revenge. Milly had to know that her act would have those consequences.

Am I saying, then, that *The Wings of the Dove* is not a Jamesian novel? It is not committed to the authority of the 'point of view' or 'post of observation'. Such authority is recognized when a reader assumes that what is presented from a privileged post of observation is to be accepted as true. The narrator of this novel mostly presents maybes and perhapses, wanderings, possibilities, everythings, pluperfect subjunctives. James's brother William couldn't abide such a form of fiction and demanded of his brother that he speak out and have his characters say what they have to say without fuss. Henry replied that he would rather die than write such a novel. But there is another way of interpreting the equivocations of *The Wings of the Dove*, by thinking of the free indirect style as the device by which James undermines the authority of the post of observation. Bourdieu has praised Flaubert as the supreme adept of such undermining:

> This distance from all positions that favours formal elaboration – it is the work of form which inscribes it into the work itself. It is the pitiless elimination of all 'received ideas,' all the typical commonplaces of any group and the stylistic traits marking or betraying adherence to or support for one or another of the attested positions or position-takings; it is the methodical use of a free indirect style that leaves as indeterminate as possible the relationship of the narrator to the facts or persons of which the tale speaks. But nothing is more revealing of Flaubert's point of view than the *very ambiguity of viewpoint* marked in the composition so characteristic of his books, and so it is with *Sentimental Education*, which critics have often reproached for being

made out of a series of 'bits put together,' by virtue of the absence of a clear hierarchy of details and incidents. As Manet will do later, Flaubert abandons the unifying perspective taken from a fixed and central point of view in favour of what one could call, with Panofsky, an 'aggregated space,' meaning a space made of juxtaposed pieces and without a privileged point of view.[39]

The *Sentimental Education*, according to Bourdieu, is a novel 'from which the author is effaced (though like Spinoza's God he remains immanent and coextensive with his creation)'.[40]

Bourdieu's reading of Flaubert is suggestive in relation to *The Wings of the Dove*. James, the author, is not dead. He is the absent God who has handed over the administration of the world to the human race, represented by the narrator, fallible and short-sighted as he may be. This prompts me to correct a point in my account of the book. The narrator, through the equivocations of the free indirect style, reports not what characters would say if each of them were managing his or her own narrative, but what he thinks these people should say. He may – for all we know – be wrong, so we have to assess his version just as strictly as the actions he reports. Bourdieu thinks of Flaubert as a bourgeois man of his time who hates the bourgeoisie, but there is no reason to think of James in this way. He had reservations about the social group to which he belonged, but they don't call for universal repudiation. The styles of *The Wings of the Dove* – for we should not reduce them to one – do not coincide with those attributable to any class, unless we call him a bohemian, an aesthete, a stylist within the intelligentsia, a coterie or an affiliation rather than a class.

Money is the question, spoken or not. We never learn how much is required.

Even in *The Portrait of a Lady*, where so much depends upon *how much*, Osmond is not poor, he need not find a job. All we learn from *The Wings of the Dove* is that a journalist's salary is not enough for marriage, though it is plenty for love. In a notebook reference to *The Wings of the Dove* James says that 'from the moment a young man engages himself he ought to have means: if he hasn't he oughtn't to engage himself.'[41] The dreadful haggling between Densher and Kate in the second volume, book eight is caused by Densher's replacing talk of money by talk of sex:

'I'll tell any lie you want, any your idea requires, if you'll only come to me.'

'Come to you?'

'Come to me.'

'How? Where?'

She spoke low. But there was somehow, for his uncertainty, a wonder in her being so equal to him. 'To my rooms, which are perfectly possible, and in taking which, the other day, I had you, as you must have felt, in view. We can arrange it—with two grains of courage. People in our case always arrange it.' She listened as for the good information, and there was support for him—since it was a question of his going step by step—in the way she took no refuge in showing herself shocked. He had in truth not expected of her that particular vulgarity, but the absence of it only added the thrill of a deeper reason to his sense of possibilities. For the knowledge of what she was he had absolutely to *see* her now, incapable of refuge, stand there for him in all the light of the day and of his admirable merciless meaning.[42]

Whose mind has produced the last three words, with an air of admirable merciless meaning? They don't sound like Densher's, which is rarely as grandiose. That leaves only the narrator's, who often sounds as if he would have done a better job if he had taken the whole story into his own hands.

Leaving the last grumpy sentence aside, what have we? The novel is, on Densher's part, a story of sin and repentance. Kate has led him into temptation. He has fallen into lies and deception, but Milly's holiness – the sight of it – has saved him. Her will, the money, the turn she has given, could be played – if this were a play – as a saintly act of revenge, though Densher doesn't take them as that. Besides, not knowing her letter, he can't know enough. He will work out his life as a Fleet Street journalist.

Kate won't live as straightforwardly as that. In the notes for the novel, James sends her off to marry Lord Mark, but he recanted that device, and there is no sign of it in the novel. We can only guess, if we care to, what she will do: go back to Aunt Maud, presumably, and wait for a man of substantial means to come to Lancaster Gate and appease her bruised will.

The passages I have quoted from the novel are so highfalutin that they may turn our minds away from the story, its lurid quality. The whole novel is propelled by two sins: first by Kate's dreadful plan by which Densher will seduce Milly and wait for her to die, leaving him a heap of money; second, by Densher's pestering Kate, in Venice, to sleep with him, else he will leave Milly alone and go back to London. His threat works:

It had simply *worked*, his idea, the idea he had made her accept; and all erect before him, really covering the ground as far as he could see, was the fact of the gained success that this represented. It was, otherwise, but the fact of the idea as directly applied, as converted from a luminous conception into an historic truth.

Admittedly, these ruminations are part of 'this prime afterglow', but even in that condition Densher knows that he made Kate accept the bargain and pay magnificently the price he had laid down. For the next twenty days he occupied himself by keeping still, being nice to Milly, choosing innocent topics of conversation and mulling over several casuistries – till the evening on which he heard from one of the gondoliers that the signorina padrona was not receiving. The 'brute', Lord Mark, has tattled, has blown the whistle on the lovers. I'm not sure that I would have blown it.

The Ambassadors

The word 'adultery' does not appear in *The Ambassadors*, though the deed and the relation do. It is quaint that we have these but not the name. In place of the absent word we have 'intimacy', a well-established euphemism, since the seventeenth century, for sexual intercourse. James gives this word a positive colour rather than a worldly or a punitive one by associating it with acts of generosity. What some call adultery is then deemed meritorious because it is committed by the right people; it seems to obey a higher law than any moral commandment. Whether one can become a right person if not such already is clear enough: one can't. If I want to join the sexual elect, I am frustrated – I must remain an aspiring lout. In 'The Story In It', Mrs Dyott and her lover Colonel Voyt are right people, socially upper class, so the question of how they acquired that privilege hardly arises, even though he has a wife with whom he lives. And in *The Ambassadors*, if a wonderful French countess, married but living apart from her dreadful husband, falls in love with a charming, reasonably well off, ten-years-younger American of Bohemian inclination, and he to some degree with her, they are free to become lovers in Paris without incurring social disgrace. But they must be careful not to offend. They do not go about together, or show themselves in the best restaurants. Their freedom, such as it is, can't be assumed abruptly, especially if the governing intelligence, Lambert Strether's, comes from Woollett, Massachusetts, where such irregular behaviours are not allowed. But Strether's morality is beginning to change. He is in Paris, the great good place, not Boston.

We have not enough evidence to call James an immoralist. On the rare occasions on which he addressed the issue of his faith, he spoke of himself as an atheist, but there are atheists and atheists. Some deny the existence of God – any God – and are scathing in the denial. Others put the question of God within the discreet seclusion of parentheses and determine to leave it alone there. James added to his atheism a steady objection to any of the organized religions, especially to Christianity. His relation to dogmas was to demand why such things should be promulgated and on what authority. He seems to have resented the obduracy of institutions and to have directed the fluidity of his imagination against them for that reason. Call him a secularist, one who finds his values endorsed or refuted by his sense of the visible world, the desires and strivings of people at large. He did not recognize any appeal beyond the evidence of his senses, 'the authenticity of concrete existence', as he called it in the preface to *The Ambassadors*: any such appeal was a psychological aberration, interesting only as such, as in 'The Jolly Corner' and *The Turn of the Screw*.

But even if we agree that James did not accept the authority of churches, it does not follow that

'anything goes'. Instead of religion, he acknowledged taste as a secular force, a god without
thunder, a social observance he often called tact,
manners or style, 'elementary undiscussable taste'
as he referred to it in 'Crapy Cornelia'. Not that it
is always undiscussable. At the end of that story,
White-Mason tells Cornelia that, no, he doesn't
want to marry her, but he wants to settle with her
beside her fireside every day for the rest of his life.
Readers are free to discuss this arrangement. In
some novels James put enough stress on certain
unattached words – usually verbs – so that they
testify to a virtual doctrine without the embarrassment of giving it a name.

The verb 'to live' often does this work, as in
the preface to *The Ambassadors* and the second
chapter of Book Fifth, where, according to James,
the essence of that novel is located:

> Live all you can; it's a mistake not to. It
> doesn't so much matter what you do in par-
> ticular so long as you have your life. If you
> haven't had that what *have* you had? … I'm
> old—too old at any rate for what I see.

> What one loses one loses; make no mistake
> about that.[1]

The version of that sentiment in the novel is more elaborate, but it sings the same tune. James was inspired when he heard that William Dean Howells gave the same advice to his invalid friend Jonathan Sturges, in Paris too. The advice is ambiguous, unless it means that it is better to have your life rather than not, but what to live means we may go read in the stars.

James did not do readers of *The Ambassadors* a favour by sending us so directly to the verb 'to live' and giving it to Strether to insist on. 'It doesn't so much matter what you do': excuse me, it does. On a wiser day, in the preface to *The Golden Bowl*, he wrote that 'as the whole conduct of life consists of things done, which do other things in their turn, just so our behaviour and its fruits are essentially one and continuous and persistent and unquenchable, so the act has its way of abiding and showing and testifying, and so, among our innumerable acts, are no arbitrary, no senseless separations'.[2] The reiteration of 'and' testifies to his insistence on the chain of values, under whatever secular names. The other things that are done 'in their turn' imply a certain logic, a sequence of proprieties, enough of which together constitute a moral life without incurring the blame of that adjective.

In Book Fourth Chapter 2, Little Bilham answers Strether's question about Chad: 'Why isn't he free if he's good?' Answer: 'Because it's a virtuous attachment.' The answer satisfies Strether, at least for a while, especially when he tells himself that Chad's virtuous attachments are none of his business. But he should have paid more attention to Little Bilham's words when he quizzes him again about the virtuous attachment linking Chad and Madame de Vionnet:

'I can only tell you that it's what they pass for. But isn't that enough? What more than a vain appearance does the wisest of us know? I commend you,' the young man declared with a pleasant emphasis, 'the vain appearance.'[3]

Strether, we read, 'looked more widely round, and what he saw, from face to face, deepened the effect of his young friend's words. "Is it so good?" "Magnificent."'[4]

The *OED* has a category for 'vain' which allows us to say that someone is vain about her hair or her voice, someone else is vain about his French, phrases not often heard nowadays but recoverable. Presumably what Strether saw in every face was the effort of each to put its best face forward, such images to be taken in default of any rationally ascertainable truth about the individual. These are vain appearances in their relation to vanity, but in social life they are often the only evidences we have. That consideration still doesn't get over the problem of 'pass for', since to pass for virtuous is to lack the virtue. Strether lets Little Bilham's second sentence wipe out his first.

Another reading of the novel, which James did not urge us to practise but which seems to me to have at least minor force, would construe it as concerned with a deplorable social pattern, which James, at least for the time being, took as a fact: that a woman who falls in love with a man tends to love him more drastically than he loves her – especially if she is refined by nature and he only a latecomer to refinement. Marie de Vionnet's love of Chad is the most blatant instance of that misfortune. Maria Gostrey's love of Strether is a less hectic version only because she prudently keeps a little distance from him: she knows that he mainly finds her agreeably useful. Strether can't avoid loving Marie de Vionnet and, if Chad were to abandon her, might well be drawn to her need. The relation between Mamie and Chad hardly arises: they are not in love. Nor does that between Mrs Newsome and Strether arise: she is only socially at hand, and besides, it takes only a week or two of Paris to convince him that he must not marry her. That leaves Maria Gostrey, at the end, who loves him more than he loves her, so his excuse for going back to the nullity of Woollett is fudge: 'Not, out of the whole affair, to have got anything for myself.' That is selfish, though it sounds selfless. The disproportion between man and woman in love has at least the value of a subplot.

Among the large events in Gloriani's garden (Book Fifth Chapter 2) there is a minor one worth remembering. Chad brings Madame de Vionnet out from the house to meet Strether. They agree to find a bench for a talk. Before much can be said, Madame de Vionnet is approached by a lady and two gentlemen. She speaks to the lady, countess to duchess, but doesn't introduce Strether. One of the gentlemen takes Madame de Vionnet off and the party of four leave Strether to his sole self. He feels that he has been treated with a want of ceremony. Has he? I think not. Madame de Vionnet wants to keep him to herself rather than spread the company to several inconsequences. Strether is not downcast: on the contrary, 'he had been overturned into the upper air, the sublimer element with which he had an affinity and in which he might be trusted a while to float'. *The Golden Bowl* and the other late novels often intuit that upper air, as if James sometimes tired of social detail and wanted to let his favourite character sit down quietly and read a page or two of Emerson. After five minutes alone, Strether is joined again by Little Bilham and in next to no time he releases his famous outburst about living life while it offers and the sadness of being too late to catch the train. Strether looks around, sees the lady at whose side Madame de Vionnet has quitted him and Gloriani approaching her with conversation, which will be witty and worldly, Strether assumes. He says to Little Bilham: 'I know—if we talk of that—whom *I* should enjoy being like!' Little Bilham thinks it is Gloriani, but Strether says no, it is Chad. At that moment, Chad comes along, bringing with him Madame de Vionnet's delightful daughter Jeanne, whom he introduces to Strether in elaborately ambiguous terms:

> And this, my dear, is the best man in the world, who has it in his power to do a great deal for us and whom I want you to like and revere as nearly as possible as much as I do.[5]

The great deal could be money, a large dowry or a determination to keep the happy couple – mother and her lover – in Paris, three thousand miles away from Woollett.

What we know of Chad, or what we are encouraged to believe of him, such that Strether envies him his life, is that he is a man of the world – at ease there – a young Pagan, marked out by women, with many good friends, 'a man to whom things had happened and were variously known', a man with a virtuous attachment to Marie de Vionnet. He knows how to enter a box in a theatre.

These attributes are enough to excite a middle-aged man's envy. The main purpose of the afternoon in Gloriani's garden is to present Strether with a variety of Parisian faces, each with its own story to tell if he will listen. The only misstatement – if it is not a lie – is Maria Gostrey's telling him that Madame de Vionnet has brought Chad up for her daughter. That turns out not to be true: Jeanne marries a real French aristocrat.

My favourite small episode in the novel is the *déjeuner* in the restaurant on the Left Bank to which Strether brings Madame de Vionnet. They met by happy chance in the great cathedral, Notre Dame. She had perhaps come to pray and sat 'within the focus of the shrine'. He sat halfway down the nave, not to pray but to let the spiritual atmosphere of peace suffuse him. Leaving together, she suggests a walk around the great church, to see it right from the outside. He invites her to *déjeuner* at a little restaurant on the Left Bank, an easy walk away. She is pleased to be his guest. She knows the restaurant only by repute. No, she does not go about with Chad in public: 'I never have such chances—not having them otherwise.' The occasion is exactly right: a table for two, an open window, 'the bright clean ordered water-side life' coming in, their *omelette aux tomates*, the bottle of straw-coloured Chablis, their human questions and answers.

Madame de Vionnet sets a decent limit to their conversation. Is Maria still away, and doesn't he miss her tremendously?

> There were reasons that made him by no means sure, yet he nevertheless answered 'Tremendously'; which she took in as if it were all she had wished to prove. Then, 'A man in trouble *must* be possessed somehow

of a woman,' she said; 'if she doesn't come in one way she comes in another.'

'Why do you call me a man in trouble?'

'Ah because that's the way you strike me.' She spoke ever so gently and as if with all fear of wounding him while she sat partaking of his bounty. '*Aren't* you in trouble?' ...

'I'm not in trouble yet,' he at last smiled. 'I'm not in trouble now.'

'Well, I'm always so. But that you sufficiently know.'[6]

That is an instance of how conversations should go, one phrase – 'a man in trouble'– being enough to raise the tone and send it aloft without being offensive. The next sentence, attributed to the narrator, testifies also to Strether's sense of his guest: 'She was a woman who, between courses, could be graceful with her elbows on the table.' The conversation would have taken a different turn, though an equally engaging one, if Strether had questioned Madame de Vionnet on her dogma, 'A man in trouble *must* be possessed somehow of a woman; if she doesn't come in one way she comes in another'. What are the different ways?

The only alarming moment in the conversation comes when Madame de Vionnet says that if Chad goes back to Woollett he will 'remain for the money'. That is indeed harsh, but Strether lets it go, he doesn't respond, though he promises to see Chad through and, by the same seeing, to see his guest through. That is sufficient. The promise brings the *déjeuner* to a glowing end. It is the first moment at which the question of Strether's being in love with Marie de Vionnet might be found among the words. Later, in Book Eleventh Chapter 2, Maria Gostrey throws off a question to Strether: 'Are you really in love with her?' He replies: 'It's of no importance I should know … It matters so little—has nothing to do, practically, with either of us.' Either of us could mean you or me, but the rest of the conversation pushes it toward Madame de Vionnet or Strether.

It does not deny that he is (or may be) in love with the wonderful countess.

Everybody's favourite episode is in Book Eleventh Chapter 3.

Strether, intent on a day's idleness after three concerning months in Paris, takes a suburban train to nearly anywhere in rural France at least an hour from the city. After eighty minutes he descends by whim at a village which seems to have the right attributes: poplars, willows, reeds, an inn – the Cheval Blanc – where he may dine, a grassy hill where he could stretch himself for sleep, and a river to remind him of a landscape painting he had nearly bought one day at an art shop in Tremont Street, Boston. So he walks about and, toward evening, sits in the garden of the inn. The confidence that had gathered for him 'deepened with the lap of the water, the ripple of the surface, the rustle of the weeds on the opposite bank, the faint diffused coolness and the slight rock of a couple of small boats attached to a rough landing-place hard by'.[7] The picture, the Lambinet, is not complete until it includes the right thing – 'a boat advancing round the bend and containing a man who held the paddles and a lady, at the stern, with a pink parasol'. Strether takes them for two very happy people, 'a young man in shirt-sleeves, a young woman easy and fair, who had pulled pleasantly up from some other place and, being acquainted with the neighbourhood, had known what this particular retreat could offer them'. In less than a minute he feels that he knows the woman with the pink parasol and that the man in shirt-sleeves must be Chad. It is a prodigious chance, that Chad and Madame de Vionnet are out like himself for a day in the country and happen to meet him. To resolve the awkwardness, he waves his hat and his stick and calls out loudly. For a second he fears that, left to themselves, Chad and Marie might have cut him, but after he has helped them get ashore, 'everything found itself sponged over by the mere miracle of the encounter'. ('Sponged over' is what a painter does with one of his failed pictures, deleting the embarrassment but not entirely removing it.) So with laughter and amazement the three of them reach the inn, have a meal and set out in a cart for the

three or four miles to the railway station and the
9.20 train to Paris.

James does not tell us how the partings, in
the city, are effected, except that Strether goes to
his hotel and sits up, fully dressed, for the watches
of the night staring into darkness.

Madame de Vionnet has done well in putting
the best possible face on the event, but the lie is
evident, that they had left Paris that morning
'with no design but of getting back within the
day'. Strether can't blink the 'too evident fact for
instance that she hadn't started out for the day
dressed and hatted and shod, and even, for that
matter, pink parasol'd, as she had been in the
boat'. But as the night wore on, he kept coming
back to another feature of the show, 'the deep,
deep truth of the intimacy revealed'.

> That was what, in his vain vigil, he oftenest
> reverted to: intimacy, at such a point, was *like*
> that—and what in the world else would one
> have wished it to be like? It was all very well
> for him to feel the pity of its being so much
> like lying; he almost blushed, in the dark, for

the way he had dressed the possibility in vagueness, as a little girl might have dressed her doll.[8]

'And what in the world else would one have wished it to be like?' is given as part of Strether's thinking. He is at the sad, desperate stage of saying to himself that if Chad and Marie are indeed lovers rather than virtuously attached, they might as well enjoy themselves and make the offence, if it is one, worthwhile. He admits to himself the awkwardness all round – he felt 'the pity of its being so much like lying' – 'but Chad and Madame de Vionnet had at least the comfort that they could talk it over together'. Strether could talk of such things only with Maria Gostrey, and he was a little afraid that she would say: 'What on earth had you then supposed?' He recognized at last 'that he had really been trying all along to suppose nothing'. 'Verily, verily, his labour had been lost. He found himself suppos-ing innumerable and wonderful things.' James uses the word 'wonderful' so often and so with-holdingly in *The Ambassadors* that, as here, he sounds like a shy pornographer saying to his raincoated gathering, 'I could a tale unfold, an image proclaim, were I so minded.' What could the supposed things be that justify his calling them wonderful?

The following morning, Strether expects a letter from Chad but gets instead a *petit bleu* from Madame de Vionnet asking him please to come to see her that evening at half-past nine. She would come to him elsewhere and at his own hour if he preferred. But I think she knew that half-past nine in her house would suit him well. I still wonder: who would take a train back to the trysting village, walk up to the other inn, gather up Chad's clothes and Marie's, pay the bill and get back to Paris without any other party being a bit the wiser? Marie could take up these tasks, given a long unoccupied day, extending the awkwardness before suppressing it. Chad was not to be counted on. He was quite absent. It turned out that he had left Paris to spend a week in London, without telling Marie of his intention, such that she had to visit Maria Gostrey to see if she knew Chad's whereabouts.

These details hardly chime with Strether's assumption, the evening before, that the boat was occupied by a very happy couple. Their tryst could have been a last fling before going their separate ways, her way in tears. Half-past nine is late to begin a conversation, even in Paris.

Strether spent the day idling, lounging, smoking, sitting in the shade, drinking lemonade and consuming ices. He wondered how Madame de Vionnet would construe the occasion:

> He wouldn't have, that is, to become responsible—this was admirably in the air: she had sent for him precisely to let him feel it, so that he might go on with the comfort (comfort already established, hadn't it been?) of regarding his ordeal, the ordeal of the weeks of Sarah's stay and of their climax, as safely traversed and left behind him. Didn't she just wish to assure him that *she* now took it all and so kept it; that he was absolutely not to worry any more, was only to rest on his laurels and continue generously to help her?[9]

Strether gave a moment or two's thought to the question of punishing Madame de Vionnet for the fraud of the evening on the river, or at least of witnessing her punishing herself, but those moments had passed without leaving a trace. He still wonders how she will deal with it:

He perceived soon enough at least that, however reasonable she might be, she wasn't vulgarly confused, and it herewith pressed upon him that their eminent 'lie,' Chad's and hers, was simply after all such an inevitable tribute to good taste as he couldn't have wished them not to render. Away from them, during his vigil, he had seemed to wince at the amount of comedy involved; whereas in his present posture he could only ask himself how he should enjoy any attempt from her to take the comedy back. He shouldn't enjoy it at all; but, once more and yet once more, he could trust her. That is he could trust her to make deception right. As she presented things the ugliness—goodness knew why— went out of them; none the less too that she could present them, with an art of her own, by not so much as touching them.[10]

The good lie has never been more imperatively endorsed. We now know how to make deception right, by being an exquisite woman, better still a countess, helplessly in love with Chadwick Newsome, and have Lambert Strether trust her to have the good taste of ordaining the right relation between speech and silence. Paying tribute to her faculty of making deception right, Strether goes further and converts what other people call adultery into her gift to Chad:

> 'You've been making, as I've so fully let you know I felt,' Strether said, 'the most precious present I've ever seen made, and if you can't sit down peacefully on that performance you *are* no doubt born to torment yourself. 'But you ought,' he wound up, 'to be easy.'[11]

At this point she is free to change the subject: 'When is it you say you go?' But Strether is not yet ready to leave her. It strikes him then that she is a creature appallingly exploited, that Chad, 'the companion of mere earthly joys, of comforts, aberrations (however one classed them) within the common experience, should be so transcendently prized'. She had but made Chad what he was – 'so why could she think she had made him infinite?' 'You're afraid for your life!' Her tears could not be stopped now, and he waits in silence till she can speak. 'The only certainty is that I shall be the loser in the end.' The loss of Chad, she must mean, but not only Chad, there is also Strether:

> 'What's cheerful for *me*,' she replied, 'is that we might, you and I, have been friends. That's it—that's it. You see how, as I say, I want everything. I've wanted you too.'

> 'Ah but you've *had* me!' he declared, at the door, with an emphasis that made an end.

In Book Tenth Chapter 3 Strether has a formal meeting with Sarah Pocock in the *salon de lecture* of his hotel. The meeting is not a surprise; Waymarsh has told him she was coming. The rhetoric of the novel urges us to expect the worst of the Pococks and to think of them accordingly. But Sarah's only crime, even in Strether's eyes, is that she has refused to let Paris interfere with Woollett.

She has come to Paris as Mrs Newsome's second ambassador to make up for the failure of her first. Chad has shown her a good time, but she has not changed her values. Surely she is not much to blame. James himself is often ironic about the common assumption that a few weeks in Paris would transform a tourist into an aesthete.

As soon as Sarah has settled herself into the 'aggressive repose' in which she does nothing but wait for Strether, he realizes that she has come to receive his submission: it is her sole thought. 'The form of his submission was to be an engagement to acquit himself within the twenty-four hours.'[12] Chad will 'go in a moment if you give him the word—he assures me on his honour he'll do that'. Strether knows that Sarah is not only Mrs Newsome's voice; he knows that 'as Mrs Newsome was essentially all moral pressure, the presence of this element [in Sarah] was almost identical with her own presence'. He can hope to evade this double presence only by referring to Chad:

> 'Something has clearly passed between you and Chad,' he presently said, 'that I think I ought to know something more about. Does he put it all,' he smiled, 'on me?'

> 'Did you come out,' she asked, 'to put it all on *him*?'

This is an early stage in a conversation that Sarah thinks, with reason, she must win. She has New England on her side, a moral tradition going back, and still largely intact, to Jonathan Edwards and Puritanism. If it has lost some of its strength – we can almost hear Sarah say – because of decadents like Strether. She must also win because she commands a style of discourse just as capable as Strether's. It is James's high style, which he can distribute among several characters, but he can't invent a new version of it for each. He did not have Dickens's quality in that respect. Even when Strether thinks he has got the better of Sarah by producing a complexity from his typical resources, he is sometimes proved wrong, as when Sarah throws the word 'duty' at him as if it were definitive:

> 'What is your conduct,' she broke out as if to explain—'what is your conduct but an outrage to women like *us?* I mean your acting as if there can be a doubt—as between us and such another—of his duty?'

> He thought a moment. It was rather much to deal with at once; not only the question itself, but the sore abysses it revealed.

Not that he has much chance of dealing with the abysses in a riposte. He resorts to a manoeuvre of the high style: 'Of course they're totally different kinds of duty.' But Sarah has the better of this: 'And do you pretend that he has any at all—to such another?' His reply is not as strong as he thinks it is: 'Do you mean to Madame de

Vionnet'?[13] Speaking her name, when Mrs
Pocock would not, is an affront, though we are
told that it wasn't meant as such. Strether then
resorts to the only evidence that he thinks should
be decisive: hasn't Chad been transformed,
through Madame de Vionnet's ministry, into a
man of refinement?

> Everything Mrs. Pocock had failed to give a
> sign of recognising in Chad as a particular
> part of a transformation—everything that
> had lent intention to this particular failure—
> affected him as gathered into a larger loose
> bundle and thrown, in her words, into his
> face.[14]

Mrs Pocock's words are not a loose bundle. They
are just as compact as Strether's own. It is also
wide of the mark to think that her 'failure' to see
the new transforming good in Chad was deliber-
ate: it is the logic of Woollett enforcing itself.
The refinement that Strether sees and admires in
Chad is not a moral improvement. Refinement is
not a moral term, it is an aesthetic term. No

moralist would use it for praise. Strether's next words are just as weak:

'Why when a woman's at once so charming and so beneficent—'

'You can sacrifice mothers and sisters to her without a blush, and can make them cross the ocean on purpose to feel the more, and take from you the straighter, *how* you do it?'[15]

The conversation proceeds as a forensic battle. Strether tries to hold forth as if he were representing a certain philosophic position. The position is that a way of life may be assessed by its results. Chad is demonstrably a finer person than he ever was in Woollett, therefore the means by which he has been brought to that merit must be sufficient justification. Mrs Pocock considers Chad's development 'hideous'. He and Madame de Vionnet are evidently living in what many would still call sin – not that she uses the word:

'You take good care not to meet,' she observed in a still higher key, 'my question about their life. If you do consider it a thing one can even *speak* of, I congratulate you on your taste!'

Sarah has caught Strether on his weak side or has caught taste on its weak side, that it consorts willingly enough with evil. Taste, as a benign substitute for religion, has only the weak device of calling some behaviour bad taste. In this context it is feeble of Strether to say that private lives are none of his business. The scene of Chad and Madame de Vionnet on the river shows that Strether does not always abide by that principle.

The conversation – or rather dispute – between Sarah and Strether ends when she calls Chad's 'fortunate development', as Strether called it, 'hideous'. 'Oh if you think *that*—!' is all Strether can say. Sarah has the last words: 'Then all's at an end? So much the better. I do think that!' And the last gesture. She walks out of the *salon* and heads straight for the low victoria that had brought her from her hotel. It awaits her. She has arranged that she may bring the episode with Strether to an end at her choice moment.

He needed to see Chad, if only because a week's unannounced absence left him disconcerted. He had to say goodbye, but before saying it he had to tell Chad that 'you'll be a brute, you know—you'll be guilty of the last infamy—if you ever forsake her'.[16] Chad's immediate answer was: 'Oh rather!—if I should do anything of *that* sort. I hope you believe I really feel it.' But within a few sentences he is making protestations that haven't quite the effect of assurances: 'I give you my word of honour that I'm not a bit tired of her.' Strether hears the word 'tired' as if Chad might have spoken 'of being tired of roast mutton for dinner'. When he leaves, Chad goes with him, apparently to accompany him to his hotel:

> But there was just one thing for which, before they broke off, Chad seemed disposed slightly to bargain. His companion needn't, as he said, tell him, but he might himself

mention that he had been getting some news of the art of advertisement. With the right man to work it *c'est un monde.*[17]

'Bargain' is a sordid word, and 'advertisement' worse. Strether is anxious to make this theme go away by making it, briefly, conversible. He does not protest to Chad that the introduction of such a subject, in the context of one's saying goodbye, is a wretched breach of taste. We have been warned of this by an image of Chad:

Chad had thrown back his light coat and thrust each of his thumbs into an armhole of his waistcoat; in which position his fingers played up and down.

No sign of the Bohemian there. Strether lets the breach of taste go until Chad mentions money. Then he bursts out: 'Shall you give your friend up for the money in it?' Even then, instead of apologizing and deleting the subject, all that Chad says is: 'It's pleasant to a fellow's feelings to "size-up" the bribe he applies his foot to.'[18]

'Pleasant to a fellow's feelings' is a trivial consideration and another breach of taste, given the seriousness with which Strether has come to speak to Chad. It is plain bad manners. We can hardly avoid the thought that this Chad, the Woollett Chad, will abandon Marie de Vionnet and go home for the money and the advertising. The dismal thought occurred to Strether, two or three times, that Chad would revert to Woollett's ways as soon as he found Strether's back turned. It will soon be turned. Strether can't stay in Paris indefinitely: an ambassador must obey his master.

When Maria Gostrey asks him 'To what do you go home?' he can only answer 'I don't know. There will always be something.' When she presses him further, he says: 'But all the same I must go.' If he must, then Woollett will receive Strether, estranged from Mrs Newsome; Chad will be submissive, wealthy, gifted with a short memory; Marnie will still be the same Marnie; Sarah will hardly speak to Strether again; and Jim will be pretty much unchanged after Paris. Technically, Mrs Newsome wins, but at a cost. An intelligent citizen will notice that the social scene has changed. In Paris, Marie de Vionnet will be what she knew she would inevitably be, lost. Maria Gostrey will be bereft, but not entirely lost.

I have to construe the scene at the river as the end of the affair between the lovers. The following morning, in Paris, there is no sign of Chad. He has not told Madame de Vionnet where he is going or why or when he will be back. That morning, she sends a telegram to Strether: please come and see her at 9.30 that night.

He answers 'yes' at once. She speaks, that night, as if Chad were already lost to her. And now Strether too. He does not see her again. He sees Chad, returned from his week in London, and Chad talks deplorable tastelessness about the art of advertisements and money.

So what is the book about? Mrs Newsome sends two ambassadors to Paris to rescue her son from decadence. One, the vulgar one, is successful. The other, Strether, the barely suppressed aesthete, doesn't even try to complete his mission: enchanted by Madame de Vionnet, he changes sides, but it is too late, every possibility is glimpsed too late. I'll give Lambert Strether the last word: 'Still, one has the illusion of freedom; therefore don't be, like me, without the memory of that illusion. I was either, at the right time, too stupid or too intelligent to have it; I don't quite know which.'[19]

The Golden Bowl

On 28 November 1892, Henry James made a note of a peculiar situation he had heard of: a father and his daughter marry simultaneously – the daughter marries a young Englishman, the father an American woman of much the same age as his daughter. The father's new wife becomes 'much more attractive to the young husband of the girl than the girl herself has remained'. The young husband has known his father-in-law's wife before either of their marriages – known her and would have married her if she had had enough money. Father and daughter console each other by spending as much time together as they can. The other two resume their intimacy:

> The father marries because he's bereft, but he ceases to be bereft from the moment his daughter returns to him in consequence of the *insuccès* of his marriage. The daughter weeps with him over the *insuccès* of *hers*, but her very alienation in this manner from her husband gives the second wife, the step-mother, her pretext, her opportunity for consoling the other.[1]

On 14 February 1895 James went back to the note and remarked to himself that 'the adulterine element in the subject' might make a difficulty for his plan of publishing it as a story in *Harper's*. In the event he put it aside for many years: only in 1904 did it become *The Golden Bowl*. But it was then a different story.

Father and daughter do not marry simultaneously: Maggie Verver marries Prince Amerigo and they have a child, a boy, the 'Principino'. Four years after Maggie, her father, Adam Verver, marries Charlotte Stant. Neither father nor daughter gives the other the slightest indication of marital dissatisfaction. The daughter's main object is to spend as much time as she can *being* the adoring daughter, which leaves the Prince and Charlotte to their own devices, about which Charlotte self-servingly declares: 'Nothing stranger surely had ever happened to a conscientious, a well-meaning, a perfect pair … forcing them against their will into a relation of close contact.' The novel asks us to cheer Maggie on, to *see* what is before her, but she is too wrapped up in her father and her child – indeed as if the child were *his*. Maggie must finally give up her innocence, her daughter-hood, in order to acquire the kind of knowledge – of multiple complicities, of ambiguities, of grey instead of black-and-white values – that allows her to claim her husband.

The title of the novel comes from the Bible and from William Blake. Ecclesiastes 12: 'Or ever the silver cord be loosed, or the golden bowl be broken, or the pitcher be broken at the fountain, or the wheel broken at the cistern.'

Blake's *Book of Thel* asks:

Can Wisdom be put in a silver rod?
Or Love in a golden bowl?

But Ecclesiastes is enough: the image of a cracked or broken bowl gave James the device on which the novel turns.

The Golden Bowl was published in November 1904. James's brother William didn't rush to read it. Henry's late style irritated him, but he tackled the book a year after it came out. On 22 October 1905 he wrote to Henry about it:

> It put me, as most of your recenter long stories have put me, in a very puzzled state of mind. I don't enjoy the kind of 'problem', especially when, as in this case, it is treated as problematic (viz., the adulterous relations between Charlotte and the Prince), and the method of narration by interminable elaboration of suggestive reference (I don't know what to call it, but you know what I mean) goes against the grain of all my own impulses in writing; and yet in spite of it all, there is a brilliancy and cleanness of effect, and in this

book especially a high-toned social atmosphere that are unique and extraordinary. Your methods and my ideals seem the reverse, the one of the other—and yet I have to admit your extreme success in this book. But why won't you, just to please Brother, sit down and write a new book, with no twilight or mustiness in the plot, with great vigor and decisiveness in the action, no fencing in the dialogue, no psychological commentaries, and absolute straightness in the style? Publish it in my name, I will acknowledge it, and give you half the proceeds. Seriously, I wish you *would*, for you *can;* and I should think it would tempt you, to embark on a 'fourth manner'.[2]

There was more to this than William's saying 'leave the psychology to me'. Henry wasn't surprised, but he was dismayed by the blankness of William's reiterations:

I mean (in response to what you write me of your having to read *The Golden B.*) to try to

> produce some uncanny form of thing, in
> fiction, that will gratify you, as Brother—but
> let me say, dear William, that I shall greatly be
> humiliated if you *do* like it, and thereby lump
> it, in your affection, with things, of the current
> age, that I have heard you express admiration
> for and that I would sooner descend to a dis-
> honored grave than have written. Still I *will*
> write you your book, on that two-and-two-
> make-four system on which all the awful
> truck that surrounds us is produced.[3]

James was entirely ready to call a spade a spade,
though he rarely needed to: he preferred to look
at certain houses, pagodas, spaniels, silken ropes,
carriages, Eaton Square and Portland Place,
objects on display in *The Golden Bowl*. But the
things that matter in the novel can't be named as
briskly as these. They are feelings, desires, intimations that can't otherwise be produced than by the
fencing conversations that bring them to light or
the musings in which they are provoked to appear.
It is only by the agitation of words, as in Maggie's
case by her agitation among the words, that

characters come to learn what they feel. It is the friction of word upon word that causes a feeling to reach the state of being recognized as that feeling and not some other one. In 'Little Gidding' T.S. Eliot writes of certain sentences that they 'sufficed to compel the recognition they preceded'. So with James in *The Golden Bowl.*

If we say that this is a novel about adultery and complain, as William did, that instead of calling it adultery straight out James makes it problematic, we are reading the book against its grain in both considerations. Another novelist – Graham Greene, perhaps – might say that the novel is about the Sixth Commandment and about two characters who are in a state of mortal sin, but James was sceptical of institutions, including that of the Ten Commandments. A commandment was not a spade – it was an ideological convention to be subjected, like any other, to intellectual scrutiny. That is why James tends to keep his characters an inch short of knowledge. Fanny Assingham, in some moods, thinks Charlotte guilty; in other moods she thinks her innocent. Even after Maggie Verver has bought the golden

bowl and the shopman tells her about the Prince
and Charlotte and comes to Maggie's house where
he sees the telling photographs, even then, she
does not accuse the Prince of adultery, threaten
divorce and send for her lawyer. There is still a
space for speculation, for surmise short of definitive knowledge. In that space she can exert her
power, take charge of her marriage and redeem it.
Adam Verver achieves a feasible marriage by
letting Charlotte bring him back to American
City and a new life of patience and social emphasis. We are free to speculate about both marriages,
short of knowing anything about them.

The awkward word is 'about'. It would be a
little better to say that the book is about the
exercise of power by means of money – 'the
power of the rich peoples', as Amerigo muses to
himself while window-shopping in Bond Street:
it is about power exercised in acquisition, leisure,
travel, sex, love, marriage and lies. We are still
reading the book according to the conventions
of realism.

Realism is a form of language legitimized by
its reference. A realistic novel supposes that there

is a world out there, external to begin with and internal only later and in a few selected instances, which can be held stable by sufficiently precise acts of reference. Reference, like naming, declares that the world is full of objects sufficiently 'there' to be recognized. William James called upon his brother to make this declaration of intent, if not of faith. Henry refused. Most of the things he cared about were not things by William's designation but fictive entities, events, processes, relations caught in the act of changing from one fencing sentence to the next. The conversation between Fanny and Charlotte at the Foreign Office party is a case in point. So if *The Golden Bowl* must be called a novel, it is a novel at some outer limit of identity where the book threatens to turn into something else. James promulgates an adversary world by finding words for it, not new words but new relations among them. Indifferent to philosophy, he was enough of a philosophic idealist to give consciousness every privilege in the constitution of reality. He had no respect for objects as they might be deemed to exist independently of the act of someone's mind that summoned them to appear. He couldn't wait to have Fanny smash the golden bowl, now that it has become a nuisance to Maggie's consciousness.

But the issue is difficult. It is well understood that in language a spiritual entity may be said to have a material correlative to which it may be reduced, as Swift in *A Tale of a Tub* reduced the claims of religious transport to breath, belching and further indignities. There are no special words for supernatural or otherwise sublime experiences; there are only ordinary words, to which unusual pressure may be applied in the hope of driving them beyond themselves. That something exalted is 'nothing but' something low is an unanswerable charge.

We call the act debunking, a practice richly appealing to ironists and satirists. William James practised it, in the letter I've quoted, by saying that Henry's suggestive innuendos were much ado about little. He didn't see that Henry's method was one by which he could advert to the things and values of the common world when they served his purpose; or he could suggest a spiritual version of them by accumulating

qualifications and corrections to their compla-
cency. He could release himself from the vulgarity of references, if only by showing how little he
respected them. Or he could at any moment
revert to their lowly state, as if he witnessed with
patience their fall from grace. He could also
invent, from the resources of language, certain
states of feeling which he could show but not
otherwise name. It was characteristic of his
imagination to see things and beings as if they
were about to melt into processes, giving up their
claims to authenticity.

One result of these liberties is that *The Golden
Bowl*, as soon as we stop thinking of it as merely
and complacently a novel, takes on some of the
qualities of an allegory; its characters, whether
we accompany them to Eaton Square, Portland
Place, Matcham or Fawns, seem to live chiefly in
our sense of them as players in an aesthetic
drama: to go for a walk is to put the walker at
risk. Symbols in the book, starting with the bowl
that gives it its title, have bearing only in relation
to the several little dramas the Ververs and their
associates enact. From time to time we are made

aware of a common world going about its business. When Mrs Vance comes to visit, we assume
that she comes from somewhere and will return
there. But no sense of a common world is allowed
to compete, for interest and concern, with the
primary situations the book projects. As for
those: William James thought they should have
been called adulteries and treated accordingly.
But in *The Ambassadors* Maria Gostrey, who
should know, tells Strether that the Count and
Countess de Vionnet are not divorced: 'this
company was, as a matter of course, governed by
such considerations as put divorce out of the
question. "*Ces gens-là* don't divorce, you know,
any more than they emigrate or abjure—they
think it impious and vulgar."'[4] A judicial separa-
tion was permissible, but not divorce. I don't
know whether a wealthy American and his
daughter, living in London, would count as *Ces
gens-là* or not. London was not Paris.

We may think, while in Adam Verver's presence, of robber barons and of his wealth as having
issued, however charmingly, from some ances-
tor's brigandage. Adam is not a brigand, he is a

connoisseur, a collector of *objets d'art* which he intends placing in a museum for the edification of the citizens of American City. Nonetheless, we can think of robber barons, brigands and other predators when we find Adam, at the beginning of the book, buying the impecunious Prince Amerigo, as a gift, a wedding present for Maggie. When we read that the Prince 'was invested with attributes', we are free to think of the financial transactions which, in late Victorian London as in American City, give point to that investment. How long the thought of Adam's power of purchase stays with us as identifying him depends on our being willing to see him enhanced to the degree of being almost redeemed. When we read that the Prince 'was to constitute a possession, yet was to escape being reduced to his component parts', we wonder whether or not Adam is to be given the same privilege. It is up to James to see us through these transactions.

As for the Prince: there is no need to debunk a down-at-heel Italian prince who needs money and finds it by marrying an immensely wealthy man's daughter. The question is, how far he may go, how far he may rise above his corruption and the superstition and decay he coolly attributes to his race. 'Oh, you deep old Italians!' Fanny Assingham says. It is a question, then, how far the Prince may go toward the light, the technology, the modernity embodied in Adam Verver, adept of the American Enlightenment. The force of attraction is Maggie. She, too, may be enhanced. From the beginning, we hear of her being 'little' and 'good', her father's loving and loved child. The question in her case is what she will do when she discovers that there is corruption in the world. One of the two instances of corruption is Charlotte Stant, but she is supposedly wonderful, too, as everyone, including Maggie, keeps telling us. That makes for a further possibility. Where William James wanted Henry to call a spade a spade and an adultery an adultery, Henry insisted on his freedom to move between the accepted names of things and other possible forms of them, which he undertook to bring forward on authority entirely his own.

Suppose Maggie were to discover the adulterous relation and were to decide that her father must never learn of it. Suppose further that she were to decide not to end her marriage but to save it, hold on to her Prince and merely rid herself of Charlotte, though in fact the decision to leave London is taken first by Charlotte. Then the story would have an emphasis somewhat as follows.

Maggie comes to know that the Prince and Charlotte were once lovers and have resumed their relation despite their marriages. She subsumes the knowledge, makes it clear to the Prince but not at all clear to Charlotte that she knows their secret, and builds a new marriage to the Prince on the strength of the more formidable person she has demonstrably become. No longer merely 'little', merely 'good'. Suppose, too, that James wanted Maggie to save both marriages by talking of them as if they were already secure, the loss of them being a disaster she is not prepared to countenance. Something like this is what happens. James gives the marriages a future by allowing Maggie to pretend that their future is already safe: she has determined to treat them as if they could only be safe.

Otherwise put: the adultery is a fact, but not beyond the reach of Maggie's interpretation, which is hardly to be distinguished from her will. Maggie deals with it to her advantage in the end. She refuses to allow the fact to prevail over her sense of it as a constituent of the new relation between herself and the Prince. In this, she differs from her father. According to Fanny Assingham, near the end of the first part of the novel, Adam Verver 'has safely and serenely enough suffered the conditions of his life to pass for those he has sublimely projected'. Maggie insists on making the chief condition of her life, her husband's infidelity, minister, however startlingly, to her project. She forces past and present to become the future – her future, since she has ordained it.

Does this amount to condoning adultery? Not quite: the adultery is not allowed to be the last word or the last deed. Leavis found the equivocation morally repellent. To James, however, a situation is not entirely as it is commonly deemed to be but as it is interpreted by the parties it affects. Maggie interprets it to suit

THE GOLDEN BOWL

the values that define the future she intends
living. She is a princess who wakens herself to a
new life of knowledge and power and has to
reckon, at the end, the cost of that achievement.
She settles for decorum and, trying to convert
her decision into a conviction, feels it partly as
power, partly as dread. Decorum is the form of
her victory and of the condition she imposes on
her husband in bringing it about. She makes a
new relation upon the ground of his need of her.

It can't be as good – or as easy – as the old love
that didn't need to know itself. But it is what she
determines to do. The Prince and Charlotte have
to put up with the new conditions, money being
money. James felt confident that he could make
his last fictions not as a moralist but as a prophet.

I have been saying that James was ruefully
sensitive to the common world and to the standard axioms upon which objects in that world
were negotiated. But he did not accept that
system of evaluation, or any system in which
individual acts of consciousness were regarded
as playing a merely secondary role. He refused to
acquiesce in the social practice that issues in

fixities and definites. Indeed he was restless in the presence of images, ideas and concepts that insisted on their being decisive. He makes this clear in the preface to the New York edition of *The Golden Bowl.* That edition appeared with decorative illustrations reproducing photographs by Alvin Langdon Coburn. James felt misgiving not about the quality of the photographs but about their having to be used at all. He refers to the question of 'the general acceptability of illustrations' as a modern and clearly regrettable habit. A book that puts forward illustrative claims – 'that is producing an effect of illustration' – finds itself elbowed, he says, 'by another and a competitive process'. The novelist, as a 'manipulator of aspects', wants readers to turn his sentences into images, acting upon the given hallucinations. But James did not want to ordain those images in a reader's mind. Nor was he willing to have pictorial illustrations keep step with the images he evoked in his own medium and his own terms. Coburn's photographs were acceptable only 'through their discreetly disavowing emulation'. On that agreement, James was happy to join the photographer in a search for appropriate scenes not only for *The Golden Bowl* but for other volumes in the New York edition:

> Nothing in fact could more have amused the author than the opportunity of a hunt for a series of reproducible subjects—such moreover as might best consort with photography— the reference of which to Novel or Tale should exactly be *not* competitive and obvious, should on the contrary plead its case with some shyness, that of images always confessing themselves mere optical symbols or echoes, expressions of no particular thing in the text, but only of the type or idea of this or that thing. They were to remain at the most small pictures of our 'set' stage with the actors left out.[5]

It was crucial that the actors be left out. A photograph of Portland Place and one of the antiques stores in Bloomsbury wouldn't do any harm and might offer images cognate with those of the novel while otherwise independent of it. But James would have vetoed any suggestion of including photographs of people who would then be taken for the actors he projected. In the novel, the characters are not described. Adam Verver is small, wears a beard and a white waistcoat. But we don't know what Maggie looks like. Or Charlotte: the few details we are given, through the Prince's eyes in Chapter 3, are mainly there to sustain his saying to himself that she looked like a huntress. What the Prince looks like, apart from his blue eyes, we are not told. James is far more interested in having Maggie ask the Prince, now that they are to be married, where he would have been without his inherited archives, annals, infamies. That is a little episode we are to make something of, beside which the mere physical appearances of Maggie and the Prince are of little account.

In the matter of photographs, then, as in the matter of naming, James shows the same reluctance to 'say it *out*, for God's sake and have done with it'. He has no misgiving about the saying, provided he is not called upon to believe in an 'it' waiting stolidly to be said. He doesn't despise images – far from it – but he deplores the fixity commonly ascribed to them, their being closed off at this point to any further development they might have had. The formal rhythm of the book is one according to which something, rough or crass as it often is, is recognized as something to be done, but the actor in the case, instead of acting upon it at that moment, holds off until another form of it is divined. Not necessarily a spiritually higher form: often it is lower, abject or desperate by comparison with its first appearance. Lies are among the instruments, the negotiations, by which these developments are brought about. Nearly every character in the book lies, apparently for a greater good or a more devious wrong and often with the rotary motion, as James called it, of the ensemble. But scruples, too, are allowed to do the work of motion nearly as well as lies: scruples, observances of taste or simply – as in Maggie's ascendancy – the determination to wait for time to do its best or worst.

We need an occasion, a scene that features some of these scruples, deflections and lies as agencies in the drama of moral choice. I choose Chapter 36, Book 5 – a scene at Fawns. The party is assembled in the smoking room to play bridge. The Prince partners Charlotte against Adam and Fanny. Bob Assingham asks to be exempted, to write letters at the far end of the room. Maggie, who doesn't play cards, is pretending to read a French magazine, but she is mainly watching the players, taking in the fact of her father's wife's lover facing his mistress; the fact of her father sitting, all unsounded and unblinking, between them; the fact of Charlotte keeping it up, keeping up everything across the table, with her husband beside her; the fact of Fanny Assingham, wonderful creature, placed opposite to the three and knowing more about each, probably, when one came to it than either of them knew of either.

Maggie puts aside the magazine, wanders over to the card table, walks slowly around, looking at each player in turn, receiving from each a genial glance. Then she walks out to the terrace. Looking through the window at the bridge players, she thinks of herself in various roles: an actress, waiting offstage for her cue; one who holds the key to the mystery of each player; a master card player with all the cards – meaning all the players – in her hand; a scapegoat, required to take upon himself all the sins of the people and to go forth 'into the desert to sink under his burden and die'; a dramatist who might ordain the play as she chose:

> Spacious and splendid, like a stage again awaiting a drama, it was a scene she might people, by the press of her spring either with serenities and dignities and decencies, or with terrors and shames and ruins, things as ugly as formless fragments of her golden bowl she was trying so hard to pick up.

Knowing that 'she might sound out their doom in a single sentence', she also knows that she won't. She could create a tragedy, but her imagining herself doing such a thing is enough to show her that she can't. Meanwhile, as she walks about, she thinks of Charlotte breaking out of her cage. Charlotte, asking Bob to take her place at the bridge table, comes out to find Maggie and, after a short interval, to accost her with a question: 'Have you any ground of complaint of me?'

James, whom Leavis charged with having lost contact with life, retained enough sense of life to know that a little instance of it can go a long way. It is a warm evening, this scene at Fawns, but Maggie has brought her shawl. When the two women meet and Charlotte starts leading up to her hard question, Maggie draws the shawl around her shoulders. 'Maggie had kept the shawl she had taken out with her, and, clutching it tight in her nervousness, drew it round her as if huddling in it for shelter, covering herself in it for humility.' But when Charlotte perjures herself and Maggie deals with the lie by answering it with another one just as bold, playing her cards just as daringly as Charlotte – 'I accuse you of nothing' – she has no further need to appear small or humble. 'And she made a point even, our young woman, of not turning away. Her grip of her shawl had loosened – she had let it fall behind her; but she stood there for anything more until the weight should be lifted.' Lifted by Charlotte, not by Maggie.

It is the kind of detail an actress would think of or a director might suggest: it comes from the tradition of the well-made play. James, a failure in the theatre, respected the methods of the well-made play and as a novelist developed them further by setting them in the minds of his characters. He retained his sense of theatre, his respect for the curtain, as here at Fawns he ends the scene by having Charlotte ask Maggie to seal her statement with a kiss – 'Will you kiss me on it then?' – and by having the kiss seen by the card players, especially by the Prince and Adam Verver.

The ending of the novel has been thought difficult. Conventionally it is a 'happy ending'. Charlotte and Adam Verver have planned to go, turned to the new life of Verver's American City, where she will be the acclaimed hostess and he the wealthy connoisseur. Maggie, the Prince and their child remain in London: the farewells have been completed. What now? Maggie determines that she will never require of her husband even a word of apology. She turns her attention, and the Prince's, to Charlotte. The novel ends:

'Isn't she too splendid?' she simply said, offering it to explain and to finish.

'Oh, splendid!' With which he came over to her.

'That's our help, you see,' she added—to point further her moral.

It kept him before her, therefore, taking in—or trying to—what she so wonderfully gave. He tried, too clearly, to please her—to meet her in her own way; but with the result only that, close to her, her face kept before him, his hands holding her shoulders, his whole act enclosing her, he presently echoed: 'See? I see nothing but *you*.' And the truth of it had with this force after a moment so strangely lighted his eyes that as for pity and dread of them she buried her own in his breast.

Maggie's 'moral', presumably, is that Charlotte's being splendid means that she will have enough splendour left over to make her life in American

City the superb thing it should be – should be for herself and her husband. Maggie and the Prince will be free to live their lives together without remorse or other embarrassment. Receiving the casual phrase – 'you see' – the Prince returns it to Maggie emphatically and comprehensively: 'I see nothing but *you.*' 'The truth of it' is not clear. It may be the truth that Maggie has taken such possession of him that he has nothing more to see. Or that his seeing nothing but her epitomizes everything in the world that he might also see. 'So strangely lighted his eyes': why strangely? What is the light? 'As for pity and dread of them': the 'as' puts a space of analogy between Maggie and the motives otherwise attributed to her. 'Pity': for a husband so defeated, so bound. 'Dread': of eyes so strangely lighted, the nature of the light unknown and therefore to be dreaded. Is it, as I think, because Maggie's eyes can't meet the Prince's that she buries them in his breast? Can't, because she realizes that she has diminished him and retains him now in his defeat? Or because she doesn't feel the need to answer his light with her own?

An actress playing the role would have to decide and would have difficulty registering pity and dread in one gesture. In the novel we are left free to construe the episode as we choose, within reason; we are given more freedom than we are likely ever to have asked for. It is a matter of accountancy, a reckoning of gain and loss in each case, Maggie and the Prince.

James's rotary motion has stopped, but it is hard to say how the characters are now disposed. He leaves us in the position he ascribed to the four principals in the last chapter, a little before the farewells: 'The four of them, in the upper air, united in the firmest abstention from pressure.' James likes to leave his characters – or at least those who are up to the experience of it – in that upper air. His readers, too: how we come to that altitude, how we breathe in that air, is the substance of the book.

But there is a question of taste here. Maggie forces her father to assent to her adjectives in praise of Charlotte – 'incomparable' and 'great'. She then forces Amerigo to join in her exclamation: 'Isn't she too splendid?' Why the lies, why the force? I don't say that these passages are as tasteless as James's presentation of Father Mitchell – 'good holy hungry man' – in the pages that take time to note his 'fat folded hands' twiddling on his stomach. But are we to forget the silken noose, 'his wife's immaterial tether', the gathered lasso around Charlotte's neck, one end of which was held firmly in her husband's wrist?

Immaterial, yes, but not entirely imaginary to Maggie.

What then is the novel about, to use the dreadful word? Maggie tells us, in her conversation with Fanny (Part Sixth, Chapter 1) about the lovers: 'Yes, because they on their side thought of everything *but* that. They thought of everything but that I might think.' The lovers regard Maggie as a simple soul who would never see events as signs. But they delay so long coming back from Matcham that she employs the waiting hours learning to think. The main consequence is that she takes control of Amerigo, Charlotte and of her father. Sometimes by speaking, sometimes not, often by listening, but always by force of thinking. It is mostly an edifying spectacle.

The Sense of the Past

James started to write *The Sense of the Past* in the first months of 1900 and worked on it for a while off and on – more off than on. He took it up again in late summer and then set it aside. One of his problems was to reconcile the book, unfinished as it was, with the 'tale of terror' that William Dean Howells had suggested to him. At that stage the first two books of it and part of a third had been written. Writing to Howells on 9 August 1900, James tried to persuade himself that the problem was a question of space: if Howells would let him have 80,000 or 100,000 words, all would be well. But James had other troubles. The more he talked of terror, the more he tired of it. He had already summoned up enough ghosts to last him a lifetime. But he had committed himself, in what he had written of *The Sense of the Past*, to a conceit he thought well of:

> I haven't, in it, really (that is save in one very partial and preliminary and expository connection), to make anything, or anybody, 'appear' to anyone: what the case involves is, awfully interestingly and thrillingly, that the 'central figure,' the subject of the experience, has the terror of a particular ground for feeling and fearing that *he himself* is, or may at any moment become, a producer, an object, of this (for you and me) state of panic on the part of others. He lives in an air of *malaise* as to the malaise he may woefully, more or less fatally, find himself creating—and that, roughly speaking, is the essence of what I have seen. It is less gross, much less *banal* and exploded, than the dear old familiar bugaboo; produces, I think, for the reader, an almost equal funk—or at any rate an equal suspense and unrest; and carries with it, as I have 'fixed'

it, a more curious and interesting drama—
especially a more human one.[1]

He would do this, some years later, with more
concentration in 'The Jolly Corner'. For the
next several years he had many different preoc-
cupations – three major novels to write without
benefit of ghosts, ten short stories, two major
tours of social survey in the United States,
recurrent bouts of depression intensified by the
death of his brother William on 26 August
1910, William's letters to gather and edit, and
two autobiographical books to write. A further
immensity of work was the New York edition of
his selected fiction, which required him to read
all the earlier novels and revise them. Revision
meant making the books consistent, in the
detail of style, with the later style he was now
committed to. In 1914 he went back to *The
Sense of the Past*, revised what he had done and
dictated about sixty-five pages of notes, indicating what he had in mind and how he planned to
proceed. He then continued with the novel,
working on it irregularly until the autumn of

1915, for about two hundred pages and left off at the difficult point where 'sweet Nan Midmore' is about to dislodge her brilliant sister Molly from Ralph Pendrel's affections. The book was published in its unfinished state, edited by Percy Lubbock, with the notes in full, in 1917, a year after James's death.

What manner of fiction did *The Sense of the Past* turn out to be? Surely it turns out to be what he intended, a romance as distinct from a novel. In the preface to *The American* he worries at some length the question: why are some fictions called real and others romantic? Dismissing the vulgar causes involving tigers and beautiful wicked women, he arrives at a decent generalization: that romance is governed by the kind of experience with which it deals, 'experience liberated, so to speak; experience disengaged, disembroiled, disencumbered, exempt from the conditions that we usually know to attach to it'.[2] Applying this, with doubtful accuracy, to *The American*, he says that what he has recognized in that work, 'much to my surprise and after long years, is that the experience here represented is the disconnected and uncontrolled experience—uncontrolled by our general sense of "the way things happen"—which romance alone more or less successfully palms off on us'.[3] A few sentences later, he concedes that an artist has drugs, in which case, applied with tact, the way things don't happen 'may be artfully made to pass for the way things do'.[4] This qualification is necessary in one's reading of *The American*.

But not of *The Sense of the Past*. James's division of the work into books is arbitrary; it doesn't help us to divine the shape of the work he intended. It is better to regard it as consisting of these four parts. Part 1: Ralph Pendrel, an intelligent but rather epicene young man living in New York, has published a book, *An Essay in Aid of the Reading of History*. He is in love with Aurora Coyne, a young widow who has returned to New York after years spent in Europe with her husband, now deceased. Ralph wants to marry her. She imposes a condition. He must subject himself to the experience of Europe, indulge his remarkably keen sense of the past – the historic passion, the backward vision – and return to her;

she wants to discover what the best is that Americans can achieve by themselves. Part 2: Ralph inherits an old house in London, bequeathed to him by a distant relative who has read *An Essay* with admiration. The house, 9 Mansfield Square, is regularly let, for the weeks of the season, to Mrs Midmore, her two daughters and her son Perry. James writes of Ralph:

> He was by the turn of his spirit oddly indifferent to the actual and the possible; his interest was all in the spent and the displaced, in what had been determined and composed round-about him, what had been presented as a subject and a picture, by ceasing—so far as things ever cease—to bustle or even to be. It was when life was framed in death that the picture was really hung up. If his idea in fine was to recover the lost moment, to feel the stopped pulse, it was to do so as experience, in order to be again consciously the creature that *had* been, to breathe as he had breathed and feel the pressure that he had felt. ... Recovering the lost was at all events on this

scale much like entering the enemy's lines to get back one's dead for burial; and to that extent was he not, by his deepening penetration, contemporaneous and present? 'Present' was a word used by him in a sense of his own and meaning as regards most things about him markedly absent. It was for the old ghosts to take him for one of themselves.[5]

This apparently means that he is not to allow his consciousness to be defeated by constituents of gone time: he is to extend his consciousness, experimentally, to engage with the past as if it were present. One night he enters the house and spends hours going through its rooms: gradually he senses that he is in touch with 'a conscious past, recognizing no less than recognized'. This sense is provoked especially by a portrait, the head of a man turned away from painter and viewer. He is convinced that the man is himself. The following day he goes to see the American ambassador and tells him that he – Ralph – and the man in the portrait are to exchange personalities and experiences.

Ralph is to enter upon the experience of the past, and the man in the portrait upon that of the future. (In the event, the exchange doesn't quite take place. Ralph, in becoming the other self, never entirely gives up his own.) He enters, not with a key but a rat-tat-tat, crossing the threshold into the past.

Part 3: the year is 1820. Ralph enters, however partially, upon the experience of his exchanged self, and in that capacity is engaged to marry Molly Midmore. (They met and fell in love, each of them without a word spoken.) This third part is a sequence of conversations between Ralph and Molly, her mother, son Perry and their friend Sir Cantopher Bland – who is in love, apparently, with the other sister, Nan – who arrives unexpectedly from the country. This part tells of the Wrong Sister being displaced by the Right One. It also shows Ralph and the Midmores gradually feeling that sinister forces are surrounding them. Ralph is now in love with Nan and she with him – this kind of fiction being hospitable to swift exchanges. Nan comes to believe that Ralph is a time traveller and that instead of marrying him she should restore him to his predestined time and place, his native temporal conditions. She 'catches in the fact something in excess of it'.[6]

In this part James has to do several mutually excruciating things. He has to show that Ralph's determination to enter the past is perverse. He has tempted himself, and yielded to the temptation, to cross the threshold; not merely to imagine the past, but to constitute it, to *be* it. One aspect of the story is the treachery Ralph commits against the present, a crime he must be brought to repent. James then has to show how the scene with the Midmores starts in a mood of elegance and brio, only to end in grimaces of terror, without anything happening that could be called an explanatory event. Moods and tones have to turn upon minute disclosures, avowals not entirely convincing, little gaps and fissures where only a seamless web of goodwill would suffice.

Part 4, the conclusion, was never written. James's notes show that he knew the difficulties. Not only had he to show the right girl ousting the wrong one – not especially hard – but he had to make the relation between Ralph and Nan develop to the point at which she would sacrifice herself and have him return to 'his own original precious Present'. The difference between Nan and her sister is that Nan prefigures the modern sensibility and Molly doesn't even guess that there might be such a thing. One of the morals of the story is that we can divine of the past only such forces as anticipate our own and lead to us. Ralph must be shown as wanting to be rescued. The past is a fine place for a visit, but you wouldn't want to live there. James insists, in the notes, upon 'Ralph's insuperable and ineffaceable margin of independence, clinging taint of modernity', his 'unspeakable homesickness for his own time and place'. But Ralph is only as modern as he can't help being. His yearning for modernity coincides with James's prejudice in its favour; as in nearly every reference to Hawthorne, James would only patronize the past and condescend to its penury.

But there is another emphasis we might remark. *The Sense of the Past* is also an allegory of the artistic imagination which comes upon its material by a hunch so imperative that it feels like a stroke of destiny. The artist comes to his subject as Ralph enters the house of the imaged dead in Mansfield Square, as if something were already there, waiting for his talent. Thereafter, he proceeds upon no official plan but by a kind of tact which James calls improvisation. Ralph in the world of 1820 comes upon whatever he needs to know, as if by instinct. At one point he needs a small picture of Molly if he is to offer her evidence of his integrity, and when he puts his hand into his pocket, lo, he finds one there. His improvisation, as James says, 'gave way without fear to the brightening of further lights'. Ralph grows many of his possibilities 'from moment to moment'. The motive, which normally precedes an action, is in Ralph's case 'constituted so much more after the fact than before it'. Where do these intimations come from if not from the experience of an artist who doesn't especially know what he is doing until he has done it? James refers to it several times in this novel as legerdemain, the happy act that made an object in Ralph's pocket 'respond to the fingers suddenly seeking it'. At one point James pushes home the analogy of the artistic process:

> Aren't we perhaps able to guess that he felt
> himself for the ten elapsing seconds the most
> prodigious professor of legerdemain likely
> ever to have existed?—and even though an
> artist gasping in the act of success.[7]

But the analogy is even more particular. The
artist implied is a painter, not a novelist. Hence
the recurrence of James's emphasis upon produced surfaces, impressions, ornaments and
appearances which don't have to be completed by
any suggestion of discursive depth. At one point
James refers to 'breath after breath and hint after
hint—though whence directed who should
say—so spending themselves upon the surface of
his sensibility that impressions, as we have
already seen, were successively effaced and
nothing persisted but the force of derived
motion'.[8] In an earlier passage this force effaces
the distinction between ornament and use. The
ornamented person is Mrs Midmore, and Ralph
understands 'that he was apparently now to see
ornament itself frankly recognised as use'. Or
later, when Ralph is somehow drawing out from

Perry's face an intelligence for which there is otherwise no evidence:

> Violating nature, as might fairly seem, in the face before him, what was such a glimmer intelligence *of?*—this he asked himself while he watched it grow and while, into the bargain, he might have marvelled at the oddity of one's wanting to be impressive without wanting to be understood. To be understood simply *as* impressive—it was this that would best consort.[9]

In another passage Mrs Midmore's sensibility is identified with 'her social surface', and Ralph is made to feel that he too will have to conduct himself and win by force of manner:

> It wouldn't of course always be the same, nor would he wish it to, since that would represent the really mad grimace; but the vision of it was precious in proportion as he felt how, so remarkably, in fact so unaccountably, he should need always to work from *behind*

something—something that, look as it would, he must object to Perry's staring at in return as if it were a counterfeit coin or a card from up his sleeve.[10]

Behind what? A chosen succession of manners: this is James's way of showing that Ralph retains enough independence to bring him back to modernity when an acute need arises.

Meanwhile, in New York Aurora has had anxieties and terrors comparable to Ralph's, such that being no longer able to stand the stress, she comes out to London, as James puts it. Ralph learns of this from the ambassador, who has had an interview with the distraught woman. Ralph asks the ambassador to give Aurora a message that he wishes to see her. This summons is James's way of avoiding the platitude of a direct meeting between the two. The meeting will of course take place, according to James's notes, but offstage.

Few readers have liked this romance. On the other hand, one of the happy few was T.S. Eliot, who apparently liked it more than James's celebrated novels. In a short essay he has three perceptions worth making a note of. One:

> In one thing alone Hawthorne is more solid than James: he had a very acute historical sense. His erudition in the small field of American colonial history was extensive, and he made most fortunate use of it. Both men had that sense of the past which is peculiarly American, but in Hawthorne this sense exercised itself in a grip on the past itself; in James it is a sense of the sense.[11]

Eliot does not reveal what the peculiarly American sense of the past is. So far as I can parse the gnomic distinction between the sense of the past and the sense of the sense, it seems to mean that Hawthorne acknowledged the force of historical events for which he was not responsible – they stood out boldly, independently. James was reluctant to see this happen. He wanted to see historical events as yielding to someone's imagination. To Hawthorne, Salem was a place in which dire things were done, crimes committed, sins to be recalled in sorrow. When James wrote about Salem in *The American Scene*, the only thing he recalled was his failure to find Hawthorne's birthplace and the House of the Seven Gables.

Eliot's second perception was this:

> The really vital thing, in finding any personal kinship between Hawthorne and James, is what James touches lightly when he says that 'the fine thing in Hawthorne is that he cared for the deeper psychology, and that, in his way, he tried to become familiar with it'.[12]

Eliot has a good deal to say about the deeper psychology – I mean a few sentences – without saying what it is or was. As evidence for it, he mentions the relation, in Hawthorne and James, between one character and another. The deeper psychology is operative when characters are aware of one another:

> Compare, with anything that any English contemporary could do, the situation which

THE CORRECTION OF TASTE

> Hawthorne sets up in the relation of
> Dimmesdale and Chillingworth. Judge
> Pyncheon and Clifford, Hepzibah and
> Phoebe, are similarly achieved by their rela-
> tion to each other; Clifford, for one, being
> simply the intersection of a relation to three
> other characters.

This depends on a theory by which a fiction is a
web of interrelations among the characters, a
character being not a self but a site of aware-
nesses. The theory is more fully developed in
Virginia Woolf than in Eliot.

Eliot's third perception by my count is just as
opaque as the first and second, but it needs longer
quotation. The gist of it seems to be that James's
dealing with Hawthorne in such an early novel
as *Roderick Hudson* was crude, but it became a
true dealing with him in *The Sense of the Past*:

> The fact that the sympathy with Hawthorne
> is most felt in the last of James's novels, *The
> Sense of the Past*, makes me the more certain
> of its genuineness ... Compare the book with

The House of the Seven Gables (Hawthorne's best novel after all); the situation, 'the shrinkage and extinction of a family,' is rather more complex, on the surface, than James's with (so far as the book was done) fewer character relations. But James's real situation here, to which Ralph's mounting the step is the key, as Hepzibah's opening of her shop, is a situation of different states of mind. James's situation is the shrinkage and extinction of an idea. The Pyncheon tragedy is simple; the 'curse' upon the family a matter of the simplest fairy mechanics. James has taken Hawthorne's ghost sense and given it substance. At the same time making the tragedy much more ethereal: the tragedy of that 'Sense,' the hypertrophy, in Ralph, of a partial civilization; the vulgar vitality of the Midmores in their financial decay contrasted with the decay of Ralph in his financial prosperity, when they precisely should have been the civilization he had come to seek. All this watched over by the absent but conscious Aurora. I do not want to insist upon the

Hawthorneness of the confrontation of the portrait, the importance of the opening of a door. We need surely not insist that this book is the most important, most substantial sort of thing that James did; perhaps there is more solid wear even in that other unfinished *Ivory Tower*.[13]

Every sentence of this needs to be answered by an expostulation beginning 'Yes, but …' My own, limited to one, would draw attention to the contradiction between the contempt that Eliot brings to ideas, in the first part of this essay and elsewhere – 'Mr. Chesterton's brain swarms with ideas; I see no evidence that it thinks' – and the respect, nothing less, that he shows to ideas in the sentence about James and the shrinkage and extinction of an idea. I have had my meagre say.

The Ivory Tower

James planned *The Ivory Tower* as a novel in ten books, a satire on the moneyed America he had seen in his two long visits. He knew little about Wall Street, but he thought or hoped that he might be able to say his say without going as far south in New York City as that. In the event, he wrote only three books and the first chapter of a fourth. These were written in the summer of 1914. When the war broke out, he apparently decided that he could not write a novel supposedly set in contemporary conditions – which might not survive the war. Percy Lubbock published *The Ivory Tower* in 1917 along with the sixty-or-so pages that James dictated as notes for it.

The plan was that the novel would begin in Newport, resort of the rich, in high summer, a Sunday morning in August, then move to New York City and find its resolution in Edith Wharton's Lenox. The events were to happen within a year, no more, no less. Only Newport got itself written. In the first chapter we meet Rosanna Gaw and her dying-but-not-yet-ready-to-die father, Abel Gaw. In the notes James says that 'Rosanna has no more taste than an elephant'.[1] His own taste in presenting her is crude. He might have called her 'fat' and been done with her, but instead he heaped belittling phrase upon phrase. She is, to begin with, 'a truly massive young person', 'the large loose ponderous girl', 'her amplitude', 'a large flat grave face', '[Gaw's] big plain quiet daughter'. After these tributes, she must get her magnificence by other means. We hear once of her intelligence. In company she is indeed formidable.

James's presentation of Abel Gaw is equally prejudicial. Rosanna sees him prowling around the next-door garden, hoping to hear of Frank Betterman's death but, before those tidings, waiting to learn what the bandaged man in bed has done with his money. Gaw and Betterman, long-ago friends and business associates, have turned into enemies, despite Rosanna's attempts to restore amity between them. Gaw thinks that Betterman has swindled him, and he may be right. James puts adjectives of diminutiveness to sinister use. Rosanna sees her father 'in a low basket-chair which covered him in save for little more than his small sharp foot, crossed over a knee and agitated by incessant nervous motion'. Gaw is, in a remarkable phrase, 'a person without an alternative'. A retired businessman, he can think only in numbers. 'If he hadn't thought in figures how could he possibly have thought at all—and oh the intensity with which he was thinking at that hour!' Rosanna is still looking at him, the 'terrible little man':

> It was as if she literally watched him just then and there dry up in yet another degree to everything but his genius. His genius might at the same time have gathered in to a point of about the size of the end of a pin.[2]

Rosanna is given another simile:

> This she knew was what it meant—that her
> father should perch there like a ruffled hawk,
> motionless but for his single tremor, with his
> beak, which had pecked so many hearts out,
> visibly sharper than ever, yet only his talons
> nervous; not that he at last cared a straw,
> really, but that he was incapable of thought,
> save in sublimities of arithmetic.[3]

This is satire, and a satirist is normally exempt from considerations of taste. Swift and Pope thought that satire trumped every other value. But *The Dunciad* and *A Tale of a Tub* are satiric in the whole, not merely in the part. If they fail as satire, they fail. *The Ivory Tower* is different. It gives its magnates an occasional slap in the face, but it then moves on to social values. Rosanna is waiting to meet Graham Fielder, a sweetheart of hers who was once urged to return to America and enjoy the felicity of a splendid establishment of money and status. She urged him to reject the offer, and he did. She now feels that he should have accepted it.

At her request, the offer has been renewed by the dying Betterman and now accepted. Fielder has arrived in Newport and has had an agreeable conversation with the old man. The fact that Graham knows nothing about finance, commerce and trade is delightful to Betterman, and the main consideration in his determination to lift the young man. Rosanna is shortly to meet him. In this chapter she is moving into the company of Davey Bradham, Gussy, Cissy Foy and the other local summer friends: there are no slaps in the face.

It was James's custom to start with one or two characters, three or four as in *The Portrait of a Lady*, then to extend the social scene to characters who may or may not be crucial. This is what we mean by calling him a social novelist, even though he retained an affection for his isolates and ghosts. The introduction of a new character, or one drawn from the past, would entail a risk, or a batch of risks. Horton Vint, a voice from Rosanna's past, had asked her to marry him three years ago, a proposal she declined, but in a day or two he will arrive in Newport. He is also a friend of Graham's. Horton is a man of the world – he knows

THE CORRECTION OF TASTE

everybody and everything. After a long conversation between Graham and Horton, Graham asks him to take care of his inherited wealth and property. Horton agrees, on the gentlemanly understanding that he will not be asked to give an account of his stewardship every Monday morning. There is also the matter of Horton and Cissy Foy: they are in love, and she is poor who should by culture be rich. James gives much of this by dictation. Horton swindles Graham, makes himself rich by making Graham poor. James didn't know enough of Wall Street to write all these rascalities up convincingly. The parts of the book that rely on character and the speech of characters are as good as any other in the later fiction.

Why did James not proceed with this novel, apart from taking the easy way out of adding long notes? The sounds of war and his own state of health may be sufficient explanation, but I doubt it. It seems to me that when he looked over the typed chapters, he saw that they were not good enough, they should not survive. He had got off on the wrong note.

Afterword

Melissa Malouf

Denis Donoghue wrote his thirty-plus acclaimed books and dozens of reviews and essays with two fingers, an old typewriter to eventual computer, the latter of which he never became at ease with – indeed, as he worked on this, his last book, he grew increasingly aggravated by both the machine and his arthritic fingers. Hence the relative brevity of what are here the last two chapters. Unable to make his fingers avoid the icons that would sometimes make his text disappear, he nevertheless thought he should add another chapter. This would be on the revised 1908 edition of *The Portrait of a Lady*, which, as several other critics have noted, gives us 'a new Isabel', or in Denis's view, another 'late novel.' Unfortunately, this book, like James's last, *The Correction of Taste*, is unfinished.

Before he wrote a word, Denis had his title: *The Correction of Taste.* I winced, probably grumbled, definitely tried to talk him out of it – it was too stuffy, too out of tune with the literary times. It didn't help matters, I thought, that the phrase belongs to T.S. Eliot, from the essay 'The Function of Criticism', which Denis describes as 'a work of angry intelligence'. Eliot writes:

> No exponent of criticism … has, I presume, ever made the preposterous assumption that criticism is an autotelic activity. … Criticism … must always profess an end in view, which, roughly speaking, appears to be the elucidation of works of art and the correction of taste.

Far from stuffy, Denis writes that 'many scholars … have lived useful lives without needing the word "autotelic".'

In Eliot's essay, Denis writes, this passage 'has the force of "No Entry" or "Keep off the Grass". It would not have that force had Eliot lived long enough and acquired the patience to appreciate the criticism – much of it autotelic – of Foucault, Barthes, deMan and Derrida'.

It didn't take Denis long to acquire such patience: reading and re-reading poems, stories, novels, studying essays in the fields of criticism, philosophy, religion, linguistics, Irish history – and the *New York Review of Books*, the *London Review of Books* and *The New Yorker* cover to cover.

He rooted for Roger Federer and Bernie Sanders (he asked me to cast a notional vote for Sanders instead of Hillary in that long-ago primary) and Rachel Maddow and all of his eight children and, in these pages, for Henry James.

Patience, paying attention, wondering, elucidating without an end in view – Denis brings these practices to bear on the later novels that James's brother William thought were too demanding, too outré, too sexually complicated and whispery.

Without these chapters, I don't think we would know how often James finds his characters (and himself, the ever-present hands-off/hands-on narrator) in 'the upper air'. Nor what pleasure Denis Donoghue took in reading in that 'upper air'.

Endnotes

1. Introduction

1. T.S. Eliot, *Selected Essays* (London: Faber and Faber, 1963), p. 395.

2. Ibid., p. 32.

3. Ibid., p. 30.

4. Ibid., p. 33.

5. Ibid., p. 25.

6. Quoted in ibid., p. 27.

7. Ibid., p. 27.

8. Ibid., p.24.

9. *The Collected Writings of T.E. Hulme*, edited by Karen Csengeri (Oxford: Clarendon Press, 1994), p. 3.

10. T.S. Eliot, *Selected Prose*, edited by Frank Kermode (London: Faber and Faber, 1975), p. 33.

11. T.S. Eliot, *Collected Poems 1909–1962* (London: Faber and Faber, 1963), p. 213.

12. Henry James, *The Complete Letters 1855–1872*, edited by Pierre A. Walker and Greg W. Zacharias (University of Nebraska Press, 2006), p. 175.

13. Henry James, *Collected Travel Writings: The Continent* (New York: Library of America, 1993), p. 414.

14. Henry James, *Complete Stories 1898–1910* (New York: Library of America, 1996), p. 828.

15. Ibid., p. 846.

16. Ibid., p. 845.

17. Quoted in the introduction to *The Other House* (New York: New York Review Books, 1999), p. vi.

18. Henry James, *The Complete Notebooks of Henry James*, edited by Leon Edel and Lyall H. Powers (New York and Oxford: Oxford University Press, 1987), p. 261.

19. Ibid., p. 80.

20. Ibid.

21. Ibid., p. 81.

22. Louis Begley, introduction to *The Other House*, p. vi.

23. James, *The Other House*, p. 5.

24. Ibid., p. 295.

25. Ibid., p. 323.

26. Ibid., p. 283.

27. Ibid., p. 310.

28. Ibid., pp. 310, 324.

29. Ibid., 312.

30. Ibid., vii.

31. Ibid., p. xiii.

2. Henry James and the Great Tradition

1. Wallace Stevens, *Opus Posthumous*, edited by Samuel French Morse (New York: Knopf, 1957), pp. 87–88.

2. *Literary Essays of Ezra Pound*, edited by T.S. Eliot (New York: New Directions, 1968), p. 91.

3. Henry James, *The Question of Our Speech* (Boston: Houghton Mifflin, 1905), pp. 4 and 20.

4. T.S. Eliot, *Selected Essays* (London: Faber and Faber, 1963), p. 20.

5. Ibid., p. 17.

6. Henry James, *The Art of the Novel* (New York: Scribner, 1962 reprint), p. 101.

7. T.S. Eliot, *After Strange Gods: A Primer of Modern Heresy* (New York: Harcourt, Brace, 1934), pp. 31–32.

8. George Santayana, *Interpretations of Poetry and Religion* (New York, 1922), p. v.

9. F.R. Leavis, *The Great Tradition: George Eliot, Henry James, Joseph Conrad* (New York: New York University Press, 1963), p. 3.

10. Ibid., p. 27.

11. Ibid., p. 2.

12. Ibid., p. 9.

13. Ibid., p. 11.

14. Ibid., p. 85.

15. R.P. Blackmur, *Selected Essays*, edited by Denis Donoghue (New York: The Ecco Press, 1986), p.178.

16. Henry James, *Collected Travel Writings: Great Britain and America* (New York: The Library of America, 1993), pp. 375–376.

17. Henry James, 'Is There a Life after Death?', reprinted in F.O. Matthiessen, *The James Family: A Group Biography* (New York: Vintage Books, 1980), p. 614.

18. Leo Bersani, *A Future for Astyanax: Character and Desire in Literature* (New York: Columbia University Press, 1984), p. 138.

19. Henry James, *The Golden Bowl*, p. 515.

20. Henry James, *The Question of Our Speech* (Boston: Houghton Mifflin, 1905), p. 10.

21. James, *Collected Travel Writings*, p. 471.

22. F.R. Leavis, *The Common Pursuit* (London: Chatto and Windus, 1952), p. 231.

23. Ibid., p. 227.

24. Ibid., p. 228.

25. Blackmur, *Selected Essays*, p. 301.

26. Henry James, 'Daniel Deronda: A Conversation', *Selected Literary Criticism*, edited by Morris Shapira (Cambridge: Cambridge University Press, 1981), p. 46.

27. Henry James, *The Awkward Age in Novels: 1896–1899* (New York: Library of America, 2003), p. 778.

28. Henry James, *Essays on Literature: American Writers, English Writers* (New York: Library of America, 1984), p. 1220.

29. Henry James, *Novels: 1903–1911* (New York: Library of America, 2010), p. 977.

30. James, *Essays on Literature*, p. 1209.

31. James, *The Awkward Age*, p. 787.

32. Ibid., pp. 807–808.

33. Blackmur, *Selected Essays*, pp. 299–300.

34. James, *The Awkward Age*, pp. 918–919.

35. Ibid., p. 927.

3. The Sacred Fount

1. *Questioning Minds: The Letters of Guy Davenport and Hugh Kenner* (Berkeley: Counterpoint, 2018), Vol. I, p. 648.

2. Ibid., p. 649.

3. Hugh Kenner, *The Pound Era* (Berkeley and Los Angeles: University of California Press, 1971), p. 16.

4. *The Complete Notebooks of Henry James*, edited by Leon Edel and Lyall H. Powers (New York and Oxford: Oxford University Press), p. 88.

5. Ibid., p. 176.

6. Henry James, *Letters*, edited by Leon Edel (Harvard University Press, 1984), Vol. IV, pp. 185–186.

7. Henry James, *The Ambassadors, The Golden Bowl, The Outcry* (New York: Library of America, 2010), p. 15.

8. Henry James, *The Sacred Fount* (New York: New Directions), pp. 34, 101.

9. Ibid., pp. 18, 54.

10. Ibid., p.197.

11. Ibid., p. 34.

12. Ibid., p. 57.

13. R.P. Blackmur, *Studies in Henry James* (New York: New Directions, 1983), p.67.

14. James, *The Sacred Fount*, pp. 96–97.

15. John Ashbery claimed, justly I'm sure, that he recalled this sentence intact fifty-two years after reading the novel in 1954. He commented on the sentence in a letter of late August 2006 to Mark Ford. Cf. *PN Review* 239, Jan.–Feb. 2018, p. 48.

16. Henry James, *Collected Travel Writings* (New York: Library of America, 1984), p. 409.

17. James, *The Sacred Fount*, p. 101.

18. Ibid., p. 102.

19. Ibid., p. 104.

20. Ibid., pp. 120–121.

21. Ibid., pp. 218–219.

22. Ibid., pp. 120–121.

23. Henry James, *Complete Stories 1898–1910* (New York: Library of America, 1996), pp. 827–828.

4. The Wings of the Dove

1. Henry James, *The Wings of the Dove*, edited by J. Donald Crowley and Richard A. Hocks (New York: Norton, 1878), pp. 14–15.

2. Henry James, *The Art of the Novel* (Boston: Northeastern University Press, 1984), p. 203.

3. James, *The Wings of the Dove*, pp. 9–10.

4. Ibid., p. 13.

5. Ibid., p. 11.

6. Ibid., p. 14.

7. Ibid., p. 15.

8. Ibid., p. 14.

9. Ibid., p. 228.

10. Ibid., pp. 230–231.

11. Leo Bersani, 'The Narrator as Center in *The Wings of the Dove*', *Modern Fiction Studies* VI (Summer 1960), p. 132.

12. James, *The Wings of the Dove*, p. 15.

13. Bersani., p. 131.

14. Ibid., p. 141.

15. Ibid., p. 135.

16. Ibid.

17. Lionel Trilling, *The Liberal Imagination* (New York: NYRB, 2008), p. 63.

18. James, *The Wings of the Dove*, p. 3.

19. Ibid., p. 120.

20. Ibid., p. 369.

21. Ibid., pp. 57.

22. Ibid., p. 391–392.

23. Ibid., p. 398.

24. Ibid., p. 402.

25. Ibid., p. 57.

26. Ibid., p. 90–91.

27. Ibid., p. 199.

28. Ibid., p. 271.

29. Ibid., p. 389.

30. Ibid., p. 333.

31. Ibid., p. 344.

32. Ibid., p. 88.

33. Ibid., p. 340.

34. Ibid., p. 364.

35. Bersani, p. 141.

36. Ibid., p. 240.

37. R.P. Blackmur, *Studies in Henry James* (New York: New Directions, 1983), p. 174.

38. Ibid., p. 403.

39. Pierre Bourdieu, *The Rules of Art: Genesis and Structure in the Literary Field*, translated by Susan Emanuel (Stanford University Press: 1995), pp. 111–112.

40. Ibid., p. 112.

41. James, *The Wings of the Dove*, p. 448.

42. Ibid., p. 294.

5. The Ambassadors

1. Henry James, *The Ambassadors*, edited by S.P. Rosenbaum (New York: Norton, second edition, 1994), p. 132.

2. Henry James, *The Art of the Novel: Critical Prefaces*,
    with an introduction by Richard P. Blackmur (New
    York: Scribner's, 1962), p. 347.

3. James, *The Ambassadors*, p. 124.

4. Ibid, p. 124.

5. Ibid, p. 134.

6. Ibid, p. 179.

7. Ibid, p. 309.

8. Ibid, p. 315.

9. Ibid, p. 318.

10. Ibid, p. 320.

11. Ibid, p. 323.

12. Ibid, p. 277.

13. Ibid, p. 278.

14. Ibid, p. 279.

15. Ibid, p. 279.

16. Ibid, p. 337.

17. Ibid, p. 341.

18. Ibid., p. 342.

19. Ibid., p. 132.

6. The Golden Bowl

1. F.O. Matthiessen and Kenneth B. Murdock (eds),
    The Notebooks of Henry James (New York: George
    Braziller, Inc., 1955), pp. 130–131.

2. F.O. Matthiessen, *The James Family* (New York:
    Knopf, 1948), p. 339.

3. Ibid., pp. 339–340.

4. Henry James, *The Ambassadors*, edited by S.P.
    Rosenbaum (New York: Norton, 1994), p. 138.

5. Henry James, *The Art of the Novel*, introduction by
    R.P. Blackmur (New York: Scribner's, 1962), p. 333.

7. The Sense of the Past

1. Henry James, *Letters*, edited by Leon Edel, Volume IV (Harvard University Press, 1984), p. 158, Letter of 9 August 1900.

2. Henry James, *The Art of the Novel*, introduction by R.P. Blackmur (Boston: Northeastern University Press, 1984), p. 33.

3. Ibid., p. 34.

4. Ibid.

5. Henry James, *The Sense of the Past* (London: W. Collins & Co., 1917), pp. 47–49.

6. Ibid., p. 327.

7. Ibid., p. 133.

8. Ibid., p. 157.

9. Ibid., p. 159.

10. Ibid., p. 156.

11. T.S. Eliot: 'In Memory', *The Little Review*, August 1918, reprinted in *The Question of Henry James*, introduction by F.W. Dupee (New York: Henry Holt, 1945), p. 115.

12. Ibid., p. 115.

13. Ibid., pp. 116–118.

8. The Ivory Tower

1. Henry James, *The Ivory Tower*, introduction by Alan Hollinghurst (New York: New York Review Classics, 2004), p. 223.

2. Ibid., pp. 6–7.

3. Ibid., p. 9.